VICTORY
DISEASE

HOW GREAT NATIONS, ARMIES
and COMPANIES FAIL

MIKE ETTORE
U.S. MARINE CORPS (RETIRED)

Fidelis Leadership Group
Developing World Class Leaders

Victory Disease
How Great Nations, Armies and Companies Fail

Paperback ISBN: 978-1-7372881-5-2
Hardcover ISBN: 978-1-7372881-6-9
Ebook ISBN: 978-1-7372881-7-6

DEDICATION

This book is dedicated to the memory of Master Sergeant Tim "Griz" Martin, who was killed in action on 3 October, 1993 in Mogadishu, Somalia, while fighting alongside of his Delta Force teammates.

He was an American Soldier.

Remember him.

CONTENTS

Cover Explanation

The highest honor the Roman Empire could bestow on its military leaders was an extravagant and lavish event called the Triumph. The General being honored was referred to as the *Triumphator*, and he wore an ornate, gold-embroidered purple tunic while riding a gold-plated four-horse carriage that carried him through the streets of Rome. He was accompanied by a procession that featured some of his soldiers and displayed the prisoners and spoils brought home from the campaign.

Legend has it that as the General stood on his carriage receiving the admiration of the senators and the cheering crowd, behind him stood a slave whose task was to hold a laurel crown over his head and whisper in his ear, *"Memento mori,"* ("Remember that you too will die) to remind the conquering hero that he was still a mere mortal and to inspire him to remain humble.

INTRODUCTION

Five furious minutes on the morning of June 4, 1942 spelled doom for one of the largest empires the world had ever seen. On that day, 47 U.S. Navy dive bombers catastrophically hit three aircraft carriers of the Empire of Japan, all of which later sunk. A fourth carrier was added to the total that afternoon. After the Battle of Midway, Japan's ability to project naval power and defend an empire that spanned 3.2 million square miles—larger than the Roman and Ottoman Empires—was finished.[1][2]

Forty-six years later, another June day officially marked the decline of another sprawling empire. On June 26, 2018, General Electric Company (GE) was kicked off the Dow Jones Industrial Average, the august stock index that tracks the performance of the world's bluest blue-chip companies. GE had been on the elite list for over 110 years. Unlike the Battle of Midway, however, the event was an ending rather than a turning point. GE's stock price that day closed at $13.74—a 77% plummet from its all-time high of $60. As of this writing, the former blue-chip trades at around $6. [3][4]

Besides falls from dizzying heights, what do the Empire of Japan and GE have in common? Both suffered from victory disease, an affliction that brings down militaries, governments, sports teams, and companies alike.

Victory disease is a fairly common organizational evolution that reflects human nature. A triumph—or a string of them—breeds overconfidence, ill-conceived aggression, complacency, or some combination of these traits and others that lead to failure. Once-successful armies are defeated. Dynastic sports teams become losers. Vaunted companies go out of business or are reduced to a shadow of their former selves.

Success Breeds Success ... and Eventual Failure

The saying that "success breeds success" remains true—up to a point. Individuals and organizations that are hungry and, in some ways, insecure, gain critical confidence that leads to more wins. In sports, this can be seen when a team breaks out of a stalemate by seizing and building on momentum. It is also a characteristic of startups that obtain proof of concept for a new idea, position it correctly, and experience rapid growth. Competent people and organizations that gain confidence and execute well are a powerful force.

A study by researchers from Stony Brook University that was published in the *Proceedings of the National Academy of Sciences* (PNAS) outlined some evidence for this perception: "researchers found that early success bestowed on individuals produced significant increases in subsequent rates of success, in comparison to non-recipients of success." The results have an interesting wrinkle, though. "[T]he study also found that greater amounts of initial success failed to produce greater subsequent success." [5]

The law of diminishing returns applies to early wins. And in many cases, over time, the opposite becomes true: "success breeds failure." Or, as former Intel CEO Andy Grove wrote, "Success breeds complacency. Complacency breeds failure. Only the paranoid survive." [6]

I think that "paranoia" is probably overstated as an antidote to victory disease. "Vigilance" is a better cure.

Nevertheless, Grove's judgment is wise. The confidence gained after a series of wins can become corrosive and become overconfidence. In some cases, leaders are convinced of their invincibility and make risky decisions that lead to their rapid downfall. In others, the decline is gradual and insidious. A history of winning may cause organizational inertia, which reduces performance and dilutes the cultural and operational norms that led to success in the first place.

So, recognizing that victory disease is common and can impact the strongest organizations and leaders … how do we avoid it?

The answer is complicated and varies in different situations. But there *are* common pillars shared by strong organizations that enable them to enhance vigilance and avoid falling prey to victory disease in the first place. And the first step is understanding what causes it and the signs that it's taken root.

In this book, we will review numerous examples of victory disease in the military and business worlds, showing the similarities that felled mighty armies and companies alike. We'll also cover the symptoms and research into this phenomenon, plus provide tried-and-true steps you can use to insulate your organization—and your personal leadership—from falling prey to this condition.

In the grand scheme of things, the mere potential of succumbing to victory disease can be a somewhat flattering problem to have. It means that a military unit, company, or individual has already achieved significant success, and the leaders of these organizations genuinely believe that because they've already done it before, they can probably do it again. It is this type of thinking, however justified by previous success, that can set the stage for the onset of victory disease.

Chapter 1

JAPAN AND *GE:*
A TALE OF TWO EMPIRES

The Rise and Fall of the Japanese Empire

Victory disease is probably as old as humanity, but perhaps its most famous example is the Empire of Japan's stunning expansion and quick contraction before and during World War II. Japanese officers even coined the term victory disease: *senshoubyou*. They used the word to come to terms with how such an initially successful, mighty military eventually failed so spectacularly. Overconfidence from early victories, rosy combat reports, and an unerring belief in Japan's military and cultural superiority led to bad decision-making and eventual defeat.

Author James P. Duffy sums up the phenomenon well in *War at the End of the World: Douglas MacArthur and the Forgotten Fight For New Guinea, 1942-1945*:

> Victory in the war's initial months had come so far ahead of schedule, and at such little cost, that faith in the "Japanese spirit" obscured [military commanders'] ability to judge events realistically.[7]

The seeds of victory disease preceded the official start of World War II and Japan's war against the United States.

The Early Expansion of the Japanese Empire

In 1931, Japan started its East Asian empire in earnest by invading Manchuria. Within a year, Manchuria was "fully occupied," the Japanese had installed a puppet government, and they started to make moves into northern China.

On July 7, 1937, the Japanese Army opened fire on Chinese troops to begin the Second Sino-Japanese War. The Japanese quickly conquered Beijing, Nanking, Hankow, Canton, and numerous other areas before reaching a stalemate against Chinese Nationalist forces. But in short order, Japan had gained "possession of roughly 25% of China's enormous territory and more than a third of its entire population." Coupled with Japan's earlier annexation of Korea in 1910 and its declaration of the "New Order in East Asia" in 1938, the empire was ascendant. [8] [9] [10]

The reasons for Japan's aggressive expansion were three-fold:

1. Nationalists were fed up with Western powers' intervention in Asia and decided to dominate the region themselves.

2. The nationalists believed in Japan's cultural and racial superiority over both Westerners and other Asians.

3. Japan was and remains poor in natural resources. Petroleum, iron, rubber, coal, soybeans, and other essential materials were needed to sustain the country's industrialization, militarization, and, ultimately, its growing empire.

Taking territory in Mongolia and China gained many of the resources that were needed. But the country's aggression sparked sanctions from the United States, one of its essential trading partners.

U.S. Economic Warfare Leads to a Shooting War

By 1939, the administration of U.S. President Franklin Delano Roosevelt ended the commercial treaty with Japan that had been signed in 1911. The following year, the U.S. restricted "exports of aviation motor fuels and lubricants and No. 1 heavy melting iron and steel scrap," followed by placing an embargo on "all exports of scrap iron and steel to destinations other than Britain and the nations of the Western Hemisphere." And in 1941, the Roosevelt administration froze Japanese assets in the U.S., effectively ending all trade. The U.S. was quickly joined by the British and Dutch, whom Japan also depended on for resources "from their colonies in southeast Asia." [11] [12]

These moves were intended to cut the Japanese off from many of the supplies that were essential to their military machine, and it worked. But this economic warfare's other, supposed goal—to stop military expansion—had the opposite effect. Faced with new material shortages and wounded national pride, the Japanese militarists quickly plotted to wage war on the United States and its Western allies in the Pacific.

The decision to go to war with the U.S. was somewhat of a practical one—Japan needed to expand to obtain resources. But it was also based in Japan's arrant belief in their destiny to rule Asia, and one of their earliest symptoms of victory disease.

Japan chose to pick a fight with a country that had double its population, 17 times its national income, five times its coal production, the highest per capita worker productivity in the world, and roughly seven times Japan's war-making potential in 1937. But recent military victories in Mongolia and China along with a venerated, lopsided naval victory over Russia way back in 1905 had imbued the Japanese Army and Navy with immense confidence. [13]

Japanese war planners were not totally unrealistic, however. They recognized the odds and many knew they were unlikely to win a protracted war against the United States. Instead, they fixated on the idea of inflicting such heavy losses on the U.S. military, so quickly, that the "soft" Americans would lose interest in fighting.

Japan's entire strategy was based on its naval war doctrine of "Decisive Battle" (*Kantai Kessen*). Planners believed that if they could engage enough of the U.S. Navy in one big battle, a victory would cause sufficient damage to force America into ceasing hostilities. This idea influenced everything from Japan's attack at Pearl Harbor to its planned defense against the U.S. counterattack to subsequent moves throughout the war. [14] [15]

On December 7, 1941, the Japanese Navy launched its devastating surprise attack on the U.S. naval base at Pearl Harbor in Honolulu, Hawaii. Following the Decisive Battle Doctrine, the aim was to quickly knock out the bulk of the U.S. Pacific Fleet and limit the United States' ability to counterattack, giving Japan time to expand its territory and prepare for another decisive stroke. Japan's surprise at Pearl Harbor was complete and highly successful—on its face.

> Twenty-one ships of the U.S. Pacific Fleet were sunk or damaged. Aircraft losses were 188 destroyed and 159 damaged, the majority hit before they had a chance to take off. There were a total of 2,403 American casualties ... [including] 1,178 military and civilian wounded.[16]

> The Japanese lost only 29 planes while taking out much of the U.S. Pacific Fleet, including sinking four of its mighty battleships (four others were significantly damaged).

> But the attackers failed to take out vital repair facilities and oil storage tanks that contained 4.5 million gallons of fuel. These resources would be crucial to America's subsequent war effort: "Eventually, all but three of the ships sunk or damaged at Pearl Harbor were repaired." And, more importantly, Japan did not sink any American aircraft carriers, all of which were absent from the base. As the war in the Pacific unfolded, the carriers quickly became the most important ships of the conflict. [17] [18]

Running Wild in the Pacific

The mastermind of the Pearl Harbor attack was Admiral Isoroku Yamamoto, a brilliant commander who had spent time in the United States as both a naval attaché in Washington and as a student at Harvard University. Despite planning the bold operation, Yamamoto was reluctant to wage war on the United States and remained pessimistic about Japan's odds. "I can run wild for six months," he famously wrote. "[A]fter that, I have no expectation of success." [19] [20] [21]

Yamamoto's prediction proved to be remarkably accurate, though his pragmatism was not widely shared among leaders in the Japanese Army and Navy. On Dec. 8, 1941, the U.S. Congress voted to declare war on Japan, though it would be some time before American forces defeated Japanese forces in combat— or even stopped their expansion.

The same day as Pearl Harbor, Japanese aircraft attacked U.S. bases in the Philippines, presaging an invasion two days later that would result in the complete surrender of American and Filipino forces by May 1942. Japan also began its attack on Hong Kong and captured the territory by Dec. 25. Nearly simultaneously attacks were launched on Burma, Thailand, British Malaya, and the strategic islands of Guam, Wake Island, Makin, Tarawa, and Rabaul. And as the Western powers attempted to muster their defenses, "the Japanese had already begun their advance on the oil-rich Dutch East Indies" in December and January, and they quickly took their objectives.

Perhaps the most stunning Japanese victory in the early days of the war was the fall of Singapore, United Kingdom's primary base in the Pacific" that was "regarded as unassailable due to its strong seaward defenses." Three Japanese divisions forced 90,000 British, Australian, and Indian defenders to surrender, taking the strongpoint in only about two weeks. In just a few months after Pearl Harbor, Japan dominated the Pacific and Indian Oceans. Australia stood alone as a regional bastion of the allied Western powers: [22] [23]

The Japanese conquest of Asia and the Pacific campaign that followed was initially an overwhelming success. Repeatedly underestimated by its enemies and often outnumbered, the disciplined, highly trained Japanese forces defeated American, British, Australian and Dutch forces as well as their local allies. The sheer expansion of Japanese territory was immense. Six months after Pearl Harbor, the Japanese Empire stretched from Manchuria in the north to New Guinea's jungle-clad Owen Stanley Range in the south. In the west, the empire began at the borders of India's Assam and continued to the Gilbert Islands in the South Pacific. The Japanese Navy General Staff even debated whether they should invade Australia, though the army's heavy commitment in China nixed this plan — Tokyo barely had the forces to defend the territory it had already acquired. [24]

Preparing for Blowback and Chasing Decisive Battle

Instead of an outright invasion of Australia, the Japanese military decided to expand its defensive perimeter in April 1942. This plan to consolidate gains and prepare for the American counterattack took on new urgency after the U.S. Navy and Army conducted a surprise joint bombing raid on Tokyo.

The physical damage to Japan was slight but the psychological impact was immense. Enraged that the mainland had been attacked, military planners redoubled their efforts to extend Japan's defensive perimeter and seek out a decisive battle that would knock the United States out of the war. [25] [26]

Japan quickly launched Operation Mo, committing its entire fleet to capturing "Port Moresby, Tulagi in the Solomon Islands, New Caledonia, Fiji and Samoa. This would then cut the lines of communication from the United States, isolating Australia and New Zealand." What the Japanese didn't know, however, was that U.S. code breakers were intercepting and decoding a significant proportion of Japanese radio messages. The Americans quickly moved three naval task forces, including two aircraft carriers, to contest the operation. [27]

What followed was the Battle of the Coral Sea, which "marked the first air-sea battle in history." When the smoke cleared, the U.S. had lost one large fleet carrier, with another carrier severely damaged, along with a destroyer, an oil tanker, and 69 aircraft. The Japanese lost one light carrier, one destroyer, three minesweepers, and over 70 aircraft, and one fleet carrier and several other ships were damaged.

The outcome is now widely regarded as something of a stalemate. It was a tactical victory for the Japanese Navy. But it was also a strategic loss, as the battle marked the first time Japan had been stopped in the five months since Pearl Harbor. [28]

And a month later, this indecisive engagement would be eclipsed by the battle that sealed Japan's fate.

The Decisive Battle

The Japanese Navy turned its attention to capturing the U.S. base at Midway Island. The small coral atoll had massive strategic importance. It is about halfway between Asia and North America and only 1,100 miles from Hawaii. Capturing Midway would significantly cut U.S. supply and communication lines to Australia. And being able to launch airplanes from it would vastly expand Japan's defensive perimeter and combat power, plus enable the Japanese to consistently threaten the U.S. base at Pearl Harbor.

Beyond those aims, Yamamoto and Japanese strategists were still obsessed with forcing a decisive battle with the Americans— and the U.S. would have to commit its forces to defend or retake a base as important as Midway. Japan sent a huge carrier battle group to capture the island and destroy the U.S. fleet that included four heavy aircraft carriers. [29]

The American defenses were significantly outnumbered and outgunned; the U.S. wound up mustering only three heavy aircraft carriers to Japan's four, along various smaller ships and 115 planes that were based on Midway Island. But the American's had one significant advantage: because of their ability to decipher coded Japanese messages, they knew when and roughly where the invasion was coming. [30]

At about 9 a.m. on June 3, 1942, the Battle of Midway began when Japanese gunners fired on a U.S. reconnaissance plane that had spotted the Japanese fleet. B-17s from Midway Island attacked the invasion portion of Japan's fleet that day with little success. The following day, more B-17s launched and conducted another failed attack, followed by Japanese carrier planes hitting the Island's airfields to little effect.

The Japanese planes returned to the carriers and began refueling and rearming to hit the island again, but a Japanese reconnaissance plane spotted the U.S. fleet. In response, the commander of Japan's aircraft carrier task force, Vice Admiral Chuichi Nagumo, decided to change targets. He ordered the planes to be rearmed again, but with munitions capable of attacking the U.S. fleet rather than the base on Midway Island. As soon as all of the strike planes had returned from their attack on Midway and were rearmed and refueled, he would commit the force to destroying the U.S. carriers.

This was a fateful decision; one that was, in part, a symptom of victory disease.

First, it fulfilled the overall Japanese naval doctrine of decisive battle. Second, Japanese naval tactics were rigidly followed, and they dictated that airpower must be launched all at once. Thus, instead of sending a portion of the attack force to engage the U.S. carriers as soon as they were spotted, Nagumo waited for all of the planes to return from the attack on the island and be rearmed and refueled. This took precious time.

The U.S. carriers Hornet and Enterprise had already launched torpedo bombers, dive bombers, and fighters against the Japanese fleet, and these planes wound up limiting Japan's ability to strike back. The first waves of U.S. Devastator torpedo bombers arrived first—almost all of them were shot down by antiaircraft fire and Japanese fighter planes. But shortly afterward, a wave of U.S. Douglas SBD Dauntless dive-bombers from the Enterprise and Yorktown spotted the Japanese fleet, and the first planes engaged Japanese aircraft carriers at 10:22 a.m.

In only about five minutes, three of the four heavy Japanese carriers—the Kaga, Akagi, and Soryu—were hit by bombs and set ablaze. The damage was severe, and destroyed their ability to launch planes in a counterattack.

The remaining undamaged carrier, the Hiryu, launched two waves of dive bombers and torpedo bombers against the U.S.S. Yorktown, setting it ablaze and severely damaging it. Two days later, the Yorktown would be sunk by a Japanese submarine as the crew attempted to save the ship. But the Americans followed up their first attack on the Japanese fleet. Dauntless dive bombers conducted a strike on the Hiryu that afternoon and crippled the carrier.

The Battle of Midway continued into June 6, but it was essentially won after all of Japan's heavy carriers were crippled and could not launch airplanes. Despite attempts to save some of the ships, they were too far gone. The Japanese scuttled the Kaga and Soryu on the evening of June 4. The carriers Akagi and Hiryu were scuttled the next morning. [31] [32]

Aftermath

In just three days—or five minutes, depending on how you measure it—Japan was doomed for defeat in World War II.

The loss of four heavy carriers to America's one effectively stopped Japanese expansion and enabled the U.S. to go on the offensive. Japan also lost about 90 percent of its committed aircraft and 300 of its best pilots, many of whom had years of experience. The ships wouldn't be replaced until the last year of the war, and the experienced pilots would never be replaced.

"In the same span of time, the U.S. Navy commissioned more than two dozen fleet and light fleet carriers, and numerous escort carriers. Thus, Midway permanently damaged the Japanese Navy's striking power, and measurably shortened the period during which the Japanese carrier force could fight on advantageous terms." [33]

Eventual U.S. victory would take three bloody years, involving over 350,000 U.S. casualties, exponentially more Japanese casualties, and the detonation of two atomic bombs over Hiroshima and Nagasaki. But for the rest of the conflict, Japan was mostly in a defensive posture as the U.S. took the initiative, executing an island-hopping campaign that took U.S. forces to the doorstep of the Japanese mainland.

The Japanese military had achieved its objective of forcing a decisive battle—only, it had lost.

The Lessons of Victory Disease

I've covered this example in detail because it is the model case for Victory Disease, and the War in the Pacific created the modern term.

The combination of pride, overconfidence, and aggression is a stark example of a mighty organization sowing the seeds of its failure. The reasons for Japan's defeat are complex and numerous, but they can be summed up by being afflicted with victory disease. And that disease can be boiled down to a few crucial factors:

- A belief, especially among Japanese militarists, that the Japanese were culturally, spiritually, and militarily superior. The U.S. might have vast industrial might, but many believed that Japanese "fighting spirit" would carry the day.

- This idea caused Japan to underestimate the U.S. and pick a fight with a country with about seven times its war-making potential. The Japanese believed they could knock the "soft" Americans out of the war in a decisive victory.

- An early string of dramatic successes reinforced this overconfidence and pushed Japan further toward its decisive battle doctrine.

- That decisive battle strategy was flawed, in retrospect.

First, the Japanese considered their encryption codes unbreakable, partially due to the complexity of their language. Thus, they had no idea that the U.S. would know the invasion was coming and be waiting in ambush.

Second, the Battle of Midway and carrier warfare at the time were both associated with victories that were as much the result of good luck as the competence of the leaders and forces involved. One or two different decisions might have resulted in drastically different outcomes. Basing the fate of an empire and a war on one battle with even odds might be considered gambling rather than a well-considered strategy. But some Japanese strategists couldn't see this clearly, as they had emerged from almost every recent battle victorious.

Third, the Japanese clung to the decisive battle doctrine long after losing the initiative at Midway. For example, the Japanese Navy would later attempt a similar decisive clash at the Battle of Leyte Gulf in late 1944. Considered by many to be the biggest naval battle in history, Japan's insufficient number of ships coupled with a scarcity of experienced pilots were crushed by a much better equipped and superior U.S. force.

The Pacific War was horrific, and stands as a stunning example of how pride, overconfidence, and a track record of success can blind the leaders of a mighty organization. In the early stages of the conflict, many Japanese military leaders had supreme confidence they would succeed. Once the initiative shifted and the weight of a vastly expanded U.S. military kicked into gear, they refused to accept what is now seen as an inevitable outcome.

These are some of the factors that make Japan's efforts in World War II the perfect example of victory disease. Not only did overconfidence drive them into an arguably unwinnable fight, but pride and rigidity in their strategy caused them to continue it long after it had already proven to be ineffective.

And if there is one aspect that's shared by business organizations that fail due to victory disease, it's a lack of flexibility—refusal of leaders to accept reality and adapt appropriately and in a timely manner to the ever-changing nature of any arena in which competition of any sort is a factor.

Chapter 2

THE RISE AND FALL OF GENERAL ELECTRIC

General Electric Company (GE) isn't a nation-state, of course, and it certainly doesn't wage war or conquer territory, at least in the literal sense.

However, its status as one of the oldest and most prestigious publicly traded companies in the U.S. made it something of an "institution." GE was long considered among the bluest of the blue-chip stocks; a security that investors buy and hold because stability and steady growth seem inevitable. And like the Japanese defeat at Midway, GE's 2018 de-listing from the Dow Jones Industrial Average was a stunning turning point for a company that had long been afflicted with victory disease.

Unlike Japan's military fortunes, there were few dramatic decisions or events that marked GE's descent besides its removal from the Dow and precipitous drops in stock price. Analysts certainly can't point to five minutes that sealed the company's recent fortunes. Nevertheless, the strategy and decision-making that harmed GE share similarities with those of Japanese military leaders in World War II.

A History of Innovation

Incorporated in 1892, General Electric Company fused famed inventor Thomas Edison's Edison General Electric Company with two other companies, including the Thomas-Houston Company. In 1900, the company "founded its flagship industrial research laboratory in Schenectady, New York," which was dedicated to creating revolutionary technology.

Over the 20th Century, GE would play a role in innovations that changed the world, including the electric motors that powered the locks of the Panama Canal, vacuum tubes that enabled televisions, the first American jet engines, advanced plastics, and more. GE's consumer products became and remained ubiquitous: "There is likely something made by GE within a few footsteps of where you are sitting now." [34] [35] [36]

In 1896, GE was one of the original companies listed on the Dow Jones Industrial Average, the famed benchmark index of blue-chip stocks that serves as a bellwether for the health of America's capital markets. The company's size and profits grew along with its innovations and the role of technology in every aspect of life. By the turn of the next century, GE reported revenue of almost $130 billion, its market capitalization peaked at $601 billion, and its share price stood at $158 just before a three to one split in May 2020. In August of that year, GE was the most valuable company in the world. [37] [38]

Runaway Profit and Growth

The two decades leading up to GE's peak were dominated by one man who radically altered the company's fortunes. Legendary CEO Jack Welch took the helm in 1980 and quickly declared a new goal: instead of merely aiming to "grow faster than the economy," he set his sights on GE becoming "the world's most valuable company." [39] GE first achieved this objective by September of 1993. [40]

Welch did it with a dramatic series of internal changes and a new external focus. As I wrote in my book, *Principles of War for the Corporate Battlefield: Warfighting Lessons for Business Leaders*:

> Welch followed up on this objective with a massed attack on the corporation's existing culture, processes, and business lines that enabled a relentless campaign to grow the company and generate profits. [41]

> Welch quickly started "blowing up the bureaucracy, eliminating the formalized meetings that had long marked GE's culture, and installing a blunter, more freewheeling style that prioritized 'facing realities' over 'superficial congeniality.'" He closed, sold, or fixed any business lines that weren't market leaders, purging 71 businesses in his first two years. Welch also instituted higher employee standards, conducted significant layoffs, and focused on expanding a promising revenue source: GE Capital, the company's lending arm, wound up yielding huge profits. [42]

> *Fortune* writer Geoffrey Colvin described Welch's management style and changes as "blitzkrieg aggressiveness" and asserts that the CEO's "great achievement" was in clearly recognizing how the business world was changing. And "having seen it, [Welch] faced up to the huge, painful changes it demanded, and made them faster and more emphatically than anyone else in business." [43]

The internal changes included giving quality leaders more autonomy and power, while investing in programs and coaching systems to make good leaders even better leaders:

> In its heyday, roughly 1985 to 2005, GE's management academy was in many ways the equal of first-rate graduate schools of business in its ability to train management teams that were able to execute its plans. [44]

Externally, Welch relentlessly and methodically chased expansion and profits—successfully catching both. In addition to becoming the world's biggest company in terms of value during his tenure as CEO—with the stock's valuation exploding to *30 times* its pre-Welch worth—GE's revenue increased by almost a factor of five. [45]

There are numerous reasons for this successful expansion. But many analysts boil down GE's growth strategy under Welch to **two primary factors:**

1. GE bought other companies that were market leaders in significant industries that had few competitors.

2. The company strayed from its roots as a technology and goods giant by drastically expanding its lending arm to become one of the biggest financial services companies in the world.

Both initiatives were incredibly successful, of course. But they also sowed the seeds of the victory disease that would cause GE's eventual decline.

Big Strategy 1: Snapping up quality companies

Capitalizing on a "new pro-merger legal environment" that was prevalent in Corporate America, GE consciously expanded with what might be called an "only the best will do" strategy for acquiring (and selling) companies. Essentially, Welch cut loose underperforming business units where GE wasn't first or second in an industry and only bought other companies who were at the top of theirs.

This strategy was based on Welch's recognition that many of GE's core industrial arms "had modest organic growth prospects." The CEO knew that to achieve his audacious objectives, he had to buy *other* companies offering *different* things. [46]

GE's reach extended into many industries, including the Japanese manufacturing sector and "financial services, medical equipment, and jet engines." Welch's most famous buy was the company's acquisition of RCA Corp. for $6.28 billion, a deal which included the NBC television network and created "a global defense, communications and consumer products powerhouse with few, if any, equals." [47] [48]

And though Welch pursued buying successful companies, he wasn't hesitant to streamline them or GE's existing subsidiaries through extensive layoffs. Every year, the company "purged" about 10% of its workforce that were considered underperformers. Estimates vary based on different qualifiers, but GE laid off between 120,000 and 175,000 employees during Welch's run as CEO. This earned him the nickname "Neutron Jack," a reference to a thermonuclear bomb. [49] [50] [51]

Welch's acquisition strategy was innovative because he was an early adopter of mergers and acquisitions that capitalized on the era's availability of cheap money and a loose M&A regulatory environment. Welch knew GE needed to look outward to achieve stellar growth, and he hit that goal with a relentless buying spree of market leaders.

Unfortunately, things don't stay "innovative" forever. And this maxim set the stage for the victory disease and decline that followed GE's run of wins.

Big Strategy 2: Pushing hard into financial services

GE had roots in financial services for the better part of a century, having established the General Electric Contracts Corporation in 1932 to help sell its consumer appliances. But Welch pursued a new and aggressive expansion in the form of GE Capital, which, by 1998, was "the product of dozens of acquisitions that ... blended to form one of the world's largest financial-services organizations."

GE Capital had "27 separate businesses, more than 50,000 employees worldwide (nearly half of them outside the United States), and a net income in 1996 of $2.8 billion." Its loans spanned everything from credit cards to cars to commercial real estate to aircraft leasing to consumer goods. In a five-year period starting in 1993, GE Capital bought over 100 companies, doubling its net income, and expanding its workforce by almost a third. [52] [53]

Much like Welch had capitalized on a permissive legal environment that made mergers and acquisitions easier, this strategy leveraged the era's hot economy and "creation of an array of new [financial] instruments." [54]

This push into finance was incredibly successful. GE Capital had $160 billion of assets in 1995, $332.6 billion in 2000, and $637 billion at its post-Welch peak in 2008. And at its peak, GE Capital was responsible for about half of its parent company's profits. [55] [56]

Some analysts at the time criticized GE's use of its financial services arm to prop up its earnings, and many of the company's other business lines became dependent on it for helping customers finance products. But there was no doubt that Welch's expansion into finance benefited the company's profits and shareholders.

"By the time Welch retired in 2001, GE's annual revenue flow had increased five times over, and its stock market value had exploded from $14 billion to $410 billion," noted business correspondent Jeff Spross. [57]

Nevertheless, both GE's aggressive acquisition strategy and GE Capital's fantastic earnings set the stage for victory disease and a stunning decline for the venerable company.

New era. Similar strategy.

Jack Welch's triumph at GE made him a legend by the time he left the company. But he also said that his ultimate success would "be determined by how well my successor grows [GE] in the next 20 years." By this metric, Welch was a failure. [58]

Jeffrey Immelt, a longtime GE executive who ran the company's successful medical-imaging division at the time, replaced Welch in September 2001. And by all accounts, his 16-year run at the helm of GE was a disaster. The company lost over a third of its value before he was pushed out of the role in 2017, a decline that only grew worse the following year when the company was de-listed from the Dow. [59] [60]

Immelt is widely criticized for the company's performance, as well as shareholder claims of misuse of a corporate jet, mis-reported financial statements, Immelt's wildly expensive severance package, and the inattention to the company's underfunded pension plan, which was described as a "$31 billion ticking time bomb" that was left for his successor. GE's success and failure periods line up almost exactly with their two respective leaders—a winning Welch and a losing Immelt. [61] [62]

But in some respects, Immelt was dealt a bad hand. The September 11th, 2001, terrorist attacks happened immediately after he took the helm, leaving "several of G.E.'s major business lines battered." And the unprecedented 2007-2008 financial crisis cratered the economy and the lending market at a time when GE Capital was responsible for over half of its parent company's revenue. Events of this magnitude would have tested the most competent of CEOs, including Jack Welch. [63]

But where GE and Immelt bear significant responsibility is their failure to adapt to changing realities, a "stay-the-course" and even "double-down" strategy that exposed the company to risk and underperformance.

In this respect, Immelt and other top GE executives had a lot in common with Japanese military strategists. And while GE's difficulties and their causes are complex, the best examples are the two strategies that made the company so innovative and successful under Jack Welch:

Strategy 1 Failure: Buying Market Leaders Stopped Working

Welch's aim to grow GE by purchasing quality companies worked well—perhaps too well, in that it spawned imitators. By the time Immelt took over in 2001, the strategy had arguably played itself out. As more companies adopted it, the competition for acquisitions and their selling prices rose, making it harder to achieve clear-cut ROI.

Despite this competition, Immelt's GE continued the strategy. As I wrote in *Principles of War for the Corporate Battlefield: Warfighting Lessons for Business Leaders:*

> Immelt went on a $175 billion buying spree of companies, many of which were overpriced, had underperformed, or subsequently failed. Among them were subprime mortgage companies that expanded GE Credit immediately before the Great Recession. Otherwise, the most notable failures involved spending "billions buying into the energy and power markets at their peaks," capped by purchasing the power and grid business of the French company Alstom for $13.7 billion in 2015. Before the sale, Alstom's 2014 Annual Report had reported "excess capacity in developed markets." And perhaps predictably, the market for its gas turbines cratered after GE's purchase was finalized. [64] [65] [66]

Failing to adapt this strategy—or GE's objective of perpetual, dramatic growth—is a clear symptom of victory disease. Professor James E. Shrager of the University of Chicago Booth school of business sums up the failure well:

> The lesson here is clear. However big you are, however successful you are today, however thoroughly you dominate your sector, plan for a time when your current strategy no longer works. Change always happens, and this means that strategies must be renewed and revised. Corporate leaders need to ask themselves: What is the pipeline? What is driving growth? What are we going to run out of? [67]

Strategy 2 Failure: Doubling Down on Financial Services Set the Stage for Disaster

Immelt and GE might have been the victims of an unprecedented financial crisis in 2008, but the decisions leading up to the event exposed the company to unprecedented risk. Author and journalist John A. Byrne describes the impact while arguing that Immelt "destroyed [the] GE he inherited:"

> Within Welch's GE, there was an accepted belief that GE Capital, the company's highly successful financial arm, should never exceed 40 percent of GE's profits or revenues. This was thought to be a delicate balance, the ideal level to enhance the industrial businesses and to retain the company's once pristine Triple-A credit rating. Undaunted, Immelt grew it to 55 percent of the company's portfolio, just at the onset of the Great Recession, ignoring this long-held belief. It didn't work all that well. [68]

Ironically, GE had continued a practice that had served it well in the previous decade while straying from the strategy that created a century of success. Instead of focusing on technological innovation, the company dove headfirst into the cheap money and new financial products—including subprime mortgages—that ended up wrecking the economy.

Victory Disease and the Failure to Adapt

Think back to Japan in the first half of 1942. At its peak, the Japanese Empire spanned roughly 3.3 million square miles, larger than the Roman or Ottoman Empires. The Japanese military had experienced a string of virtually unbroken victories for the last 11 years—arguably since its stunning victory over Russia in 1905. Military planners believed in the superiority of Japan's naval forces, soldiers, air power, and fighting spirit, and pursued a Decisive Battle Doctrine that had served them so well in the past.

In 2000, GE was in a similar situation. The company had expanded to become the most valuable company in the world, with a market capitalization hitting $601 billion and stock prices 30 times what they were before 1980. The company had "conquered" and integrated hundreds of other companies in a string of most successful acquisitions that drove this growth, while betting big on financial services, a play that yielded immense profits.

Japan hit a decisive moment at the Battle of Midway that drastically changed its fortunes within months, whereas GE's critical setback—the 2008 financial crisis—took eight years. And while Japan was totally defeated in only three years, GE's stunning "defeat" of being de-listed from the Dow happened 18 years after its peak. Nevertheless, the arcs were similar in that the both institutions suffered from overconfidence and a stay-the-course mentality that hastened their decline.

Japan's belief in its military superiority and fighting spirit paid off until it didn't. And its Decisive Battle Doctrine worked until it encountered a determined enemy on which it didn't—and wouldn't, even if the Imperial Navy had triumphed at Midway. By the war's conclusion in 1945, U.S. war production numbers had become staggering and the American public's desire for total victory remained high. Similarly, GE's acquisition strategy worked until it didn't; other companies had changed the equation by making winning deals harder to find. Nevertheless, both GE and Japan stuck to the playbook of what had worked in the past.

Further, Japan's Decisive Battle Doctrine gambled heavily on a single engagement in a type of warfare where a few crucial decisions could tip the scales either way. And military planners didn't account for the unexpected occurrence of US intelligence breaking Japanese codes and setting up an ambush. At its heart, the battle and the doctrine that drove it were a big risk that led to disaster. Likewise, GE's decision to increase its dependence on risky financial instruments—simply because it had worked in the past—was a huge gamble for a diverse, multibillion dollar company. And it ended in business catastrophe.

Both GE and the Japanese Empire were afflicted with victory disease. And their ultimate failures are directly tied to symptoms of the condition: overconfidence and an inability to adapt to changing circumstances.

These aren't the only symptoms of victory disease, and we'll cover more of them in this book. But making assumptions based on past success and failing to make crucial adjustments are near the top of the list.

Chapter 3

OVERCONFIDENCE IN SOMALIA

The United States may have benefited from Japan's affliction with victory disease in World War II, but US military and political leaders have also fallen prey to the condition. Vietnam and Afghanistan are lengthy case studies in overestimating America's strategic will to win long wars. A handful of smaller conflicts have shown the limits of US resolve and ability to accomplish its objectives, as well.

In the early 1990s, the US and the United Nations became embroiled in the decades-long Somali Civil War. And what started out as a straightforward peacekeeping mission ended up as a strategic loss, severely testing America's prestige in a conflict that didn't directly affect national defense.

The Somali Civil War is still an ongoing fight that started in 1978, after Somalia invaded neighboring Ethiopia and lost decisively. In that war's aftermath, the demoralized Somali military staged a coup against former President Mohamed Siad Barré. The effort failed but created lasting opposition groups who sought to overthrow his regime. [69]

By 1991, Siad was overthrown, Somalia became a failed state, and clans and warlords clashed in a brutal conflict that spurred a humanitarian crisis. In 1992, "an estimated 350,000 Somalis died of disease, starvation, or civil war" and up to half of the population was at risk of starvation or malnutrition. [70] [71]

The international community decided to intervene. But a 1992 humanitarian mission by the UN failed when Somali militias violated a ceasefire and hijacked food convoys intended for civilians. US President George H. W. Bush proposed backing up the mission with military force, setting the stage for a massive battle the following year. [72]

Boots on the Ground

On December 9, 1992, 1,800 US Marines arrived in Mogadishu and formed the vanguard of a 25,000-strong US-led peacekeeping force. "Operation Restore Hope" was initially a success, as the troops protected aid workers and enabled food distribution. Mass starvation was averted and security improved—for a time.

A leading Somali warlord, General Mohammed Farah Aideed, proposed a disarmament conference in May 1993, and all warring factions agreed to attend. That month, the US-led Unified Task Force (UNITAF) handed over peacekeeping operations to a UN force dubbed "UNOSOM II." Many US troops pulled out as a coalition of 21 countries and nearly 30,000 international personnel took the lead. [73] [74] [75]

These security and humanitarian gains were short-lived, however. The Somali warlords stepped up their attacks, including the shocking slaughter of 24 Pakistani troops by Aideed's forces in June. And in August, "four US Army military policemen were killed when a remotely detonated mine blew up their vehicle," while seven other US soldiers were wounded in a similar attack. [76] [77]

The UN passed a new resolution calling for greater military involvement. And the US, now under the leadership of President Bill Clinton, eventually had a new, more aggressive mission spearheaded by a new task force.

Task Force Ranger and the Hunt for Aideed

In August 1993, a "450-man elite unit commanded by US Army Major General William Garrison" arrived in Somalia. Dubbed "Task Force Ranger," it "had the mission of capturing Aideed and his key lieutenants and turning them over to UNOSOM II forces," followed by degrading his clan's ability to fight UN forces. [78]

Several factors before Task Force Ranger's arrival made this specific mission—and, ultimately, achieving stability in Somalia—very difficult and likely impossible. Nevertheless, US politicians and military planners either didn't recognize the severity of these issues or believed they could overcome them.

Task Force Ranger got off to a rocky start with its first 'snatch-and-grab' mission targeting Aideed's clan on August 30th. Troops conducted a helicopter assault on suspected clan hideout but instead detained nine UN employees. Clinton administration officials and US military leaders were embarrassed by the failure and increased the pressure on Garrison and Task Force Ranger to quickly succeed in their mission.

Five raids that followed in September had mixed success. While Task Force Ranger captured "Aideed's chief financier," the warlord himself had gone underground, and Garrison recognized that capturing Aideed himself would be "highly improbable." In addition, despite diversionary measures designed to confuse the warlords about Task Force Ranger's operations, the Somali fighters were able to spot patterns in the first six missions and prepare for the seventh. Among other factors, this knowledge set the stage for the most intense US battle since the Vietnam War. [79]

The Battle of the Black Sea

On October 3, a Somali spy working for Task Force Ranger reported "that senior members of Aideed's Habr Gidr clan planned to meet that afternoon in the Bakara Market region of south Mogadishu." Garrison and his officers quickly formulated a plan to raid the meeting and make arrests.

The plan followed the general pattern of some of the previous missions. Sixteen helicopters would insert a combination of about 100 Delta Force special operators and US Army Rangers at and around the clan's suspected meeting place. Delta operators would hit the target and capture the clan leaders while Ranger blocking forces set up a cordon around the area to cut off enemy reinforcements. Several helicopters would then orbit the scene, providing sniper and gunship cover, overhead intelligence, and a search and rescue capability. As the prisoners were being secured, a ground convoy of Humvees and three five-ton trucks would be on its way into the city from Task Force Ranger's base to extract everyone. The mission was supposed to be a surgical, 'in-and-out' operation.

Things went according to plan, at first. Delta operators quickly secured the building and 24 prisoners. Ranger forces successfully set up blocking positions despite one soldier being seriously injured while fast-roping from a hovering helicopter. The ground convoy arrived at the scene on time and loaded up the prisoners. [80]

But then, things quickly went south:

- US forces encountered fierce resistance from Somali fighters that was greater than they'd experienced on any of the previous six missions.

- Somali fighters set up numerous roadblocks in the city in an attempt to cut off US backup and escape.

- One of the orbiting MH-60 Black Hawk helicopters was shot in the tail rotor by a rocket-propelled grenade (RPG) and crashed "approximately four blocks northeast of the target building ... killing both pilots and injuring several soldiers in the cargo compartment of the aircraft." [81]

The loss of the helicopter changed the mission *instantly*. Rescuing the downed US personnel and securing the crash scene became a priority over extracting Somali prisoners and the initial US ground forces.

Part of the Ranger blocking force moved to the crash site on foot and were joined by a Combat Search and Rescue (CSAR) force inserted by helicopter, which also evacuated two seriously injured soldiers. Mission commanders also re-tasked the main ground convoy to the crash site, instructing ground commanders to secure it before leaving the city. But the convoy had started taking numerous casualties from intense enemy fire, and more men had moved to the crash site on foot.

US forces were under pressure, disorganized, and spread out. And within minutes, Somali gunmen shot down another helicopter in the city.

From Bad to Worse

This story has been immortalized by the book and movie *Blackhawk Down*, as well as numerous after-action reports, news articles, and documentaries. Every source depicts an intense, chaotic struggle. Essentially, a surgical capture mission rapidly evolved into a massive battle where US forces fought for survival, trying to escape a city that had largely turned against them.

Two Delta Force operators, Master Sergeant Gary Gordon and Sergeant First Class Randall Shughart volunteered to be inserted by helicopter to defend the second Blackhawk crash site. They did so heroically before being overrun and killed by a mob of Somali gunmen, actions for which both men posthumously received the Medal of Honor. The lone survivor of the crash, Chief Warrant Officer-2 Michael Durant, was taken captive and held prisoner by Aideed's clan before eventually being released after the battle on October 12.

The rest of the force weathered an intense and confusing gunfight that lasted until the next morning. The convoy holding the Somali prisoners was unable to make it to the first helicopter crash site and took casualties after encountering heavy resistance. So, the convoy and elements of a quick reaction force they ran into on the way home had to return to base. Another rescue effort also attempted to reach the first crash site but was turned back by withering small arms fire.

Meanwhile, the Rangers and Delta operators who had reached the first downed helicopter on foot were surrounded and running low on supplies. Throughout the evening of October 3rd, helicopters dropped them water and ammunition while a steady stream of gunships raked the city with rockets and bullets to prevent the position from being overrun. Meanwhile, General Garrison and other commanders worked for hours to assemble a UN/US relief force of more than 60 vehicles. Crucially, this convoy included Malaysian armored personnel carriers and Pakistani tanks that could protect the troops from Somali small arms.

Lead elements of the armored rescue force made it to the first crash site by about 2 a.m., helping defend it as soldiers worked to free the body of a dead pilot. Another relief force eventually arrived at the second downed Blackhawk, but "no trace could be found of the lost soldiers and aviators." Finally, all US and UN wounded and remains were put in the armored personnel carriers and evacuated out of the city at dawn, while much of the ground force had to follow them out on foot. This harrowing run through a hostile city to a rally point at a local stadium was dubbed "the Mogadishu Mile." [82] [83]

The Battle of Mogadishu, aka the Battle of the Black Sea, was finally over. It was the most violent battle the US military had experienced since the Vietnam War—and it shocked the American public. US forces suffered 19 men killed, 73 wounded, and one captured, while their Malaysian and Pakistani allies suffered two killed and nine wounded. Estimates of Somali losses vary from 350 to 1,000 militiamen and civilians killed and thousands more wounded. [84]

In the battle's immediate aftermath, one US aviator, Michael Durant, was still held captive by forces loyal to Aideed. And shocking footage of the bodies of Delta operators Gary Gordon and Randall Shughart being dragged through the streets of Mogadishu were broadcast throughout the world.

On a more personal level, my friend, Tim "Griz" Martin was killed during this battle while fighting alongside his Delta Force teammates. Griz had a dynamic, fun loving personality that endeared him to all, and his death shook even the most hardened warriors of his tribe. His family and friends still mourn the loss of this exceptional father, husband, and warrior.

A Pyrrhic Victory and the Elements of Victory Disease

Despite the surprising, chaotic clash, high casualties, and loss of several helicopters, General Garrison initially viewed the mission as a successful step in Task Force Ranger's ultimate mission: to degrade the clans' ability to fight. While US forces had weathered significant casualties, they had also successfully captured their targets, escaped the city, and inflicted far more damage on the enemy. Nevertheless, Garrison's initial assessment didn't account for the battle's impact on public sentiment and US politics.

The number of dead and wounded on both sides and the images of dead Americans dragged in the streets shocked the US public and political class. Within two days after the battle, President Clinton decided to withdraw all forces by March 1994. As US Army Major Timothy Karcher wrote in a paper assessing the operation, "The US had essentially lost in Somalia" despite a "tactical victory."

Karcher "singles out one culprit" for why the US was strategically defeated: "the victory disease."

> [A]n arrogant belief in the superiority of US forces coupled with a complacent underestimation of the opponent, resulted in defeat at Mogadishu. The members of TF Ranger used already established patterns that allowed the Somalis to seize the initiative and then inflict significant casualties upon the United States, ultimately forcing us to withdraw in defeat.

An inherent belief in the "superiority of US forces" and underestimating the clans may have been the overall reasons the US was caught off guard and strategically defeated. But this case of victory disease also had several specific warning symptoms before the battle. Crucial issues that imperiled the mission were either missed, poorly understood, or not judged serious problems:

- Several months prior to Task Force Ranger's arrival, US reconnaissance efforts had determined "the capture of Aideed was possible" because of his public movement. But that assessment officially changed before Task Force Ranger got there when the warlord went underground in response to heightened attacks by UN forces. Nevertheless, the capture mission went forward in August. [85]

- The U.N.'s and U.S.' fight against the warlords and their clans drastically changed local perception of the international mission. In particular, a helicopter gunship attack that killed between 20 and 73 Somalis at a clan meeting on July 12, 1993 sparked popular outrage. As *The Washington Post* reported that December:

  > *"The attack caused an outcry among U.N. civilian staffers, exposed rifts among U.N. member states contributing troops to the Somalia operation and plunged the United Nations into a full-scale guerrilla war in which Aideed made Americans his primary target."*

  This change in perception meant that US forces weren't just fighting some clan fighters on October 2–3; *they were fighting a significant portion of a city.* [86]

- US political leaders wanted quick, clean results from Task Force Ranger but hesitated to provide overwhelming support—and they did not follow through on the political and military objectives after experiencing a bloody battle. For example, no AC-130 gunships that could provide devastating fire support were available to ground forces during most of the task force's deployment. Nevertheless, the political pressure to capture Aideed and his lieutenants quickly (and relatively bloodlessly) was intense before the

Battle of the Black Sea … and evaporated almost instantly after it.

There are other reasons that the battle's intensity was a surprise, including poor synchronization between radio communications and overhead surveillance and a mistaken belief that Somali fighters couldn't take out helicopters with unguided rocket-propelled grenades. But the overarching reason for the surprisingly violent clash and the strategic defeat that followed remains overconfidence.

The political goals and a belief that US forces could enter a hostile city and surgically capture and extract clan leaders weren't realistic. In hindsight, an expectation that the military could do it almost bloodlessly was absurd. Victory disease was in full effect.

Chapter 4

WHEN GREAT RETAILERS STUMBLE

If the United States were a company, it would still be considered a successful one so far. Despite sometimes falling
prey to victory disease in wars like Afghanistan and Vietnam
and smaller conflicts like Lebanon and Somalia, none of those
outcomes were an existential threat. The US has suffered
strategic failures, often lost prestige on the world stage, and
continually experiences internal political discord, but has
continued to remain a relatively stable nation. Thus, if the
US government or military were a publicly-traded company,
it wouldn't have yet been kicked off the Dow Jones Industrial
Average like GE.

There are actual companies that fit this narrative of severe challenge and recovery, of course:

Ford Motor Company lost a record $12.7 billion in 2006 as
it struggled to retain market share and undertook a dras-
tic reorganization process to stop its obvious death spiral.
Ford succeeded in this effort, bouncing back to weather the
Great Recession better than many of its major competitors.
Nevertheless, a looming subprime auto loan issue coupled
with a pandemic, supply chain issues, and Ford's large debt has
some analysts speculating that the company may be in for hard
times again. [87] [88] [89] [90]

As I write this in March of 2022, Apple is an unrivaled technology titan and is the most valuable company in the world, with a market capitalization of 2.75 Trillion USD, but don't forget that it was on the edge of bankruptcy in 1997. At the time, Apple sold an "outdated" operating system, and its products were "expensive and uninspiring."

Nevertheless, the company's comeback is legendary. The return of Steve Jobs and a series of innovative product rollouts—"the iPod in 2001, the iPhone in 2007, and the iPad in 2010"—brought Apple back from the brink and more. And recently, the company's move into subscription-based services, its tightly managed ecosystem, and more innovative products like the Air Pods have kept Apple growing to stratospheric success. [91] [92]

Victory disease isn't always fatal—though it certainly can be. Other companies (and countries, for that matter) aren't as lucky or skilled as Apple. One or two major challenges or a combination of several can take a business down for good. And these falls are often accompanied by leadership's failure to recognize or adapt quickly to internal and external threats.

The Sadder Side of Sears

The venerable Sears, Roebuck and Co. was founded in 1896 as a mail-order catalog company that grew into the largest retailer of the 1980s. But by 2018, it was ranked 31st and had been bought by its retail competitor K-Mart. And the second-tallest building in the Western Hemisphere that had long served as the company's headquarters was no longer named "the Sears Tower." That year, Sears declared bankruptcy. [93]

The company's 125-year history has many innovative pivots, including a move from catalogs to stores in 1925, offering auto insurance in 1931, a shift to the suburbs in the '50s and malls in the '80s, and an expansion into consumer credit in 1986. These adaptations kept the retail giant growing, and Sears' stock price eventually achieved an all-time high of $195.18 in 2007, two years after the K-Mart merger. But even though the company hit this financial peak, the seeds of its demise were already sown. Sears' brick-and-mortar big-box competition, the unstop-pable trend of online retail, and a series of internal missteps combined to take it down. [94]

A painful retail spiral

Between 2006 and 2017, Sears' retail sales fell from $53 billion to just $14.9 billion, a 72% decline.

Longtime Sears Chairman Eddie Lampert became CEO in 2013. He attempted to rescue the company by re-focusing on re-tail and continued his previous restructuring efforts of closing underperforming stores. Many of these moves were unpop-ular and earned Lampert the title of "the Most Hated CEO in America," according to a survey by the employer review site Glassdoor. More significantly, his unpopular decisions failed to stop Sears' downward spiral. Lampert stepped down as CEO af-ter a five-year run when the company filed for bankruptcy in 2018. [95] [96] [97]

Lampert, a billionaire former hedge fund manager who still served as Sears' chairman, purchased the company in bank-ruptcy for $5.2 billion the following year. The deal saved "425 stores and roughly 45,000 jobs," but the latest version of the retail chain is a shadow of its former self. Sears Holdings now operates a fraction of its previous locations and is ranked 99th among retailers with only $3 billion in sales. [98] [99]

What caused this stunning fall?

The rise of online shopping that hurt many brick-and-mortar re-tailers is an easy narrative, but the impact of e-commerce isn't the only factor. Business reporter Shoshanna Delventhal con-vincingly argues that the company's actual decline took place over decades, labeling it "A Tale of Retail Hubris."

For example, Sears further diversified into financial services in the 1980s by purchasing "Dean Witter Reynolds Organization Inc., a stockbroker ... Coldwell, Banker & Co., a real estate broker" and rolling out the Discover credit card. Sears also dabbled in e-commerce by creating "a pre-web online portal" in partnership with IBM and CBS. While company leaders could be lauded for these innovative attempts, most of the efforts were spun off or sold by the '90s, some of them at a significant loss. [100]

The company eventually returned to its retail roots and started restructuring after the 2005 merger with K-Mart, with then-K-Mart chairman Lampert also becoming chairman of the new company. Delventhal writes about the effects of Lampert's efforts:

> In 2008, he split the company into 30 divisions—which swelled to 40 a year later—each of which reported profits separately and had to compete with the others for resources. Lampert was both strict with money and distant, seldom leaving his home in South Florida.
>
> Divisions found themselves acting like separate companies, even drawing up contracts with each other. Compensation costs rose as each division hired its own senior management. These executives, in turn, had to form their own boards, and their pay was determined according to an in-house profit metric that led to cannibalization as some divisions cut jobs, forcing others to step in. The appliances unit found itself being gouged by the Kenmore unit, so it bought wares from LG, a South Korean conglomerate, instead.

Beyond these issues, retail consultant Tricia McKinnon argues five reasons Sears failed to turn things around:

- **"A failure to keep innovating:"** while Sears was very innovative through most of its history, making business shifts that reflected changes in the country, McKinnon argues that the company's last successful innovation was the introduction of the Discover credit card in 1985.

- **"An inability to stay ahead of competitive threats:"** discount retailers like Wal-Mart undercut mid-priced retailers like Sears, winning much of their market share.

- **"A lack of focus:"** selling refrigerators and tools along with clothing in a brick-and-mortar environment—while positioning the company correctly in the minds of consumers—was a challenge for Sears.

- **"A lack of continual and sustained investment:"** McKinnon notes that Sears' competitors spent 4.5 to 16.9 times more per square foot on improving retail stores, and Sears' stores "fell further into disrepair," leading to a "negative investment cycle." In addition, Lambert sold prime company real estate for cash, spinning the properties off into a real estate investment trust.

- **"Too many missed opportunities"** included Sears starting an e-commerce push three years after Amazon while simultaneously losing focus on the stores that generated most of the company's revenue. [101]

All these arguments have merit and contributed to Sears' decline, but a failure to meet two external challenges stands out. First, online shopping put a severe dent in Sears and other brick-and-mortar retailers, though, as McKinnon notes, attributing failure to this alone is incomplete. That's where the second factor comes in: the same period in which Sears nosedived saw the rise and massive success of Wal-Mart. And overall, brick-and-mortar retail sales still dwarfed online sales.

Thus, a combination of these elements—**online retail** and **discount retail competition**—were the two main external factors that took down Sears.

The company simply couldn't sell goods cheap enough, convenient enough, or market them well enough to compete with Amazon *or* Wal-Mart. Despite selling nearly everything a home could need, Sears maintained a reputation as the place to go for power tools or appliances. In contrast, Wal-Mart or Target became the place to go for *everything*—eventually, so did Amazon. And both those options tended to be *cheaper*.

Nevertheless, Sears faced many other challenges, both external and self-inflicted. As McKinnon writes, "at some point there is a tipping point when a company fails on so many fronts it's impossible to get back up." [102]

Sears' leaders clearly fell victim to victory disease. And when they finally acknowledged the growing threats to their business model and tried to adapt, they consistently made the wrong moves.

Comparable Challenges Took Down Toys "R" Us

The Toys "R" Us story shares many similarities with the fall of Sears. Like its fellow retailer, the famous toy seller had its heyday in the 1980s and early 1990s before hitting rock bottom this century. Interestingly, Toys "R" Us once had to come back from the brink of failure to achieve its peak, but the company couldn't pull this trick off twice.

Charles Lazarus founded the business in 1948 as "a baby goods and furniture store called Children's Bargain Town in Washington, DC." Over the next decade, the company expanded its toy selection until it was renamed Toys "R" Us in 1957. Lazarus grew the organization for nine more years before selling it to Interstate Sales "to help finance a larger national expansion." Lazarus stayed on to run the new company's Toys R Us division. [103]

Unfortunately, Toys "R" Us' parent company filed for bankruptcy in 1974, and Lazarus was forced to restructure Toys "R" Us' by selling off "unprofitable divisions." The effort succeeded. Toys "R" Us went public in 1978, experiencing 16 years of immense growth and success until Lazarus stepped down as CEO in 1994. [104] [105]

By the end of Lazarus's run, Toys "R" Us was the leading toy retailer and one of the world's most famous brands:

> The company—which went public in 1978—
> helped turn a $500 million toy industry in 1950
> into one worth $12 billion in 1990. At the height

of its power, Toys 'R' Us sold 18,000 different toys in 1,450 locations around the globe and controlled 25 percent of the world's toy market. During the store's heyday, it seemed like everyone was a "Toys 'R' Us kid." [106]

By the time Lazarus retired, Toys "R" Us was a retail behemoth at the top of the toy market. But two decades of decline followed this peak. After five CEOs, losing out to Wal-Mart as the leading toy retailer, a disastrous deal with Amazon, going private followed by a failed bid to return public, an ineffective mergers and acquisitions strategy, and accumulating mountains of debt, Toys "R" Us filed for bankruptcy in 2017.

What Went Wrong?

Overall, the two things that took down Sears were also primarily responsible for the demise of Toys "R" Us: **discount retail** and **online retail** competition. But as with all corporate giants and most cases of victory disease, there were many more factors at play.

For example, overall toy sales declined as kids "shift(ed) to digital" experiences like video games. And when the retail giant attempted to turn things around while struggling under $1.86 billion in debt, a leveraged 2005 buyout of the company by the private-equity firms Bain Capital and Kohlberg Kravis Roberts only made things worse. "Immediately after the deal, [Toys "R" Us] shouldered more than $5 billion in debt." [107]

Toys "R" Us also attempted to innovate into e-commerce by partnering with one of its fiercest competitors, but the deal ultimately backfired:

> In 2000, Toys R Us entered a 10-year partnership with Amazon to be Amazon's exclusive seller of toys. The partnership stipulated that Toys R Us pays Amazon $50 million a year plus a percentage of sales.
>
> The joint toy store was successful which prompted Amazon to begin expanding its toy category.

> The giant e-commerce company also included Toys R Us competitors.

> Toys R Us ultimately sued Amazon and won, allowing the chain to terminate the deal. But the money won in court could not make up for the years it had lost in developing its own online presence and e-commerce strategy. [108]

This deal and other moves were significant factors in Toys "R" Us' march to bankruptcy. But the core of the company's failure is what it *tried to do* to compete with online and discount retail, along with what *it didn't do*.

When former CEO and Founder Lazarus renamed the company Toys "R" Us in 1957, he used an innovative strategy to crush the competition. And ironically, an updated version of this strategy eventually destroyed Toys "R" Us:

> He had an idea that was bigger than Children's Bargain Town or any kids' store he had ever seen—a massive store filled with every toy in existence. In 1957, he got out of the baby furniture business, renamed his company Toys 'R' Us and created the first ever big-box toy store.

> The new megastore took a supermarket-style approach to toy selling, which distinguished it from every other toy store in existence. Most toy stores were small and family-run, and only carried a limited line of products. Lazarus' stores, on the other hand, were orders of magnitude larger than their competitors, and presented a smorgasbord of thousands of different toys. [...]

> Lazarus bought and sold so many toys that he was able to negotiate contracts to buy toys for cheaper than his competitors. This made Toys 'R' Us into what retail historians recognize as the first "category killer"—a company that so completely dominates its retail category that it drives all of its competition out of business. [109]

At the time, this was an incredibly innovative strategy. But fast forward 50 years or so, and big-box competition was all over the place along with e-commerce options. All of them were more convenient and typically cheaper than Toys "R" Us. The company failed to innovate into digital experiences and a successful e-commerce model and couldn't beat brick-and-mortar alternatives. So, Toys "R" Us leaders decided to compete on price alone. It was a failed strategy, explains Wharton marketing professor Barbara Kahn:

> Kahn noted that Toys R Us and other category killers had business models built around offering the lowest prices and best assortments—but now Amazon dominates both of those. In order to survive, companies have to find some other differentiator. For example, Best Buy matched Amazon's prices, but also adopted a showroom model that took advantage of the fact that customers like to see, touch and try electronics, combined with the ability to get advice from knowledgeable store associates.
>
> "Best Buy appreciated that and leveraged that advantage, and through price matching, they made sure the customers who came also bought from Best Buy," Kahn said. Toys R Us failed to create compelling reasons for customers to visit, either due to a superior store experience or via partnerships to exclusively sell popular brands or products.
>
> "Toys R Us was trying to win on convenience and price, but it wasn't convenient and the prices weren't so great," she said. [110]

Ultimately, complacency about its status as a leading retailer and the toy market's stability, along with superior competition, marked the demise of Toys "R" Us. And once company leaders recognized the symptoms of victory disease, they made the wrong moves to counter it.

Former retail executive and Director of Retail Studies at Columbia University Mark Cohen argues that Toys "R" Us was "guilty of serial mismanagement:"

> "Retailers today, especially in any kind of fashion or trend segment, have to progress," he said. "They have to morph, they have to modify. They have to represent the changes in the marketplace and their customers' behavior. Toys R Us has never been able to wrap their arms around the changes necessary, and this is the inevitable outcome." [111]

Failure to innovate is almost always a precursor to the "inevitable outcome" of victory disease. It stems from complacency and overconfidence that blind business leaders to evolving threats— at least until it's too late.

Chapter 5

THE SYMPTOMS OF VICTORY DISEASE

We've covered several symptoms of victory disease in our military and business examples of the condition, chief among them are **overconfidence** and **complacency** among senior leaders. There are other symptoms, but all of them flow from these two traits. We've also applied the concept and symptoms to **organizations** *and* **people**—a *company or military* suffers from victory disease, and business or military *leaders* are afflicted with it.

The diagnosis works interchangeably because while the condition's expression is through people and their decisions, organizational groupthink takes over. In its worst, common form, victory disease is part of the company's culture, as created by the behavior of its senior leaders.

More junior leaders quickly learn that the requisite for promotion is to adopt the highly-valued conformity element prevalent in the senior leadership, which leads to a perpetuation of the status quo and the "executive echo chamber." In such an environment, those who dare challenge or attempt to change the corrosive culture are often ignored, relegated to lesser roles, or even terminated because they "don't fit in" with the existing culture of the leadership team. If they are allowed to remain, more often than not, the very type of leaders who could help a company avoid or escape from the clutches of victory disease end up frustrated, and they vote with their feet, joining companies where they'll be respected and valued.

These are general statements, of course, and victory disease can take different forms. For example, a select few leaders at the top of an org chart can easily guide an organization off a cliff, taking many competent subordinates along for the ride. Just one CEO or four-star general has immense power and responsibility. But the condition isn't usually limited to one or a handful of people. Victory disease typically infects much of the organization and its culture, perpetuating a cycle of conformity and eventual failure.

Regardless, the primary enablers of victory disease are *human* weaknesses, cognitive-emotional states expressed in individuals, and, ultimately, their organizations. They include:

- **Overconfidence** (primary symptom and cause)

- **Complacency** (primary symptom and cause)

- **Underestimating enemies/the competition** (secondary symptom)

- **Failure to collect, acknowledge, or use valuable intelligence** (secondary symptom)

Overconfidence

Overconfidence, arrogance, or hubris; take your pick. Each word has slightly different meanings, but all of them describe confidence that has strayed into dangerous territory. It's such a common symptom and expression of victory disease because many leaders and other highly successful people learn that achieving (or at least projecting) confidence is a ticket to advancement.

Both popular perception and research back up this idea—with some serious caveats. For example, the author of a study who interviewed 23 employers and "107 employees in corporations in Melbourne, New York and Toronto" found confidence clearly tied to workplace success. Further, self-confidence has been linked to enthusiasm for learning and, revealingly, whether other people *perceive someone* as competent. This latter point is crucial, as others' perceptions of an individual's competence *because of their confidence* may be one of the strongest drivers of professional advancement. [112] [113] [114] [115]

So, a healthy amount of confidence is valuable. In technicians or artists, for example, task-specific confidence, sometimes called "self-efficacy," may help them do what they do best *better*. And generally confident leaders benefit from the perception they're competent because if they're confident; others are more willing to follow them. [116]

Where confidence goes off the rails is when it evolves into overconfidence, or "self-confidence" is conflated with "self-esteem." Basically, self-confidence is an individual's belief in themselves through their abilities, and it may be higher or lower in certain situations. In contrast, self-esteem is the value you apply to yourself based on life experiences—and researchers have uncovered a possible dark side to an excessively high "self-esteem":

> Roy F. Baumeister, professor of psychology at Case Western Reserve University in Cleveland, OH, has been studying self-esteem for decades, and has published more research on the topic than any other specialist in the U.S.[...]

> "Self-esteem is, literally, how favorably a person regards him or herself," Baumeister writes. "High self-esteem can mean confident and secure–but it can also mean conceited, arrogant, narcissistic, and egotistical."[...]

> "The effects of self-esteem are small, limited, and not all good," Baumeister says. [117]

Burmeister and his colleagues conducted a thorough review of studies on the effects of self-esteem, publishing their findings in *Psychological Science in the Public Interest*. They concluded that while self-esteem was strongly *related* to happiness and some professional and academic success, it did not clearly *drive* success. "Occupational success may boost self-esteem rather than the reverse," they wrote. [118]

In contrast, researcher Laura Guillén at the Esade Business School in Barcelona found that managers with a higher sense of *self-efficacy*—the confidence to get certain things done well—are more resilient "in the face of obstacles and adversity … which ignites their career success." Nevertheless, even this generally positive trait can become a bad thing if people experience too many wins or perhaps more importantly, no failures:

> [According to] Guillén, this can lead to people becoming victims of their high self-regard. Individuals high in self-confidence may go on to exhibit self-complacency and a lack of focus which can potentially harm their results. Accordingly, this 'too much of a good thing' principle means that the positive relationship between job self-efficacy and resilience (and success) will reach a turning point, after which the association will turn negative.

> In short, too much self-confidence might hinder individuals' drive to continue to learn and invest their effort into new endeavors; it might lead to poor decision making and might even harm interpersonal relationships. [119]

Let's sum things up:

- A healthy amount of self-confidence, either general or task-specific, has positive effects, especially for individuals who specialize or lead others. It helps them complete tasks, weather challenges, and lead people effectively.

- Self-esteem that creates a sense of worth regardless of merit or accomplishment usually makes individuals happier but *not* more competent.

- Any form of self-confidence that evolves into overconfidence—often, after repeated wins—can be a destructive trait. As a good summary of Esade's research puts it, "Too low and too high self-confidence do not lead to career success." [120]

The conclusion by many in the field of psychology in regards to overconfidence closely mirror victory disease: success can drive destructive overconfidence. And all the other symptoms of the condition flow from this trait.

Bad Decisions and the Dunning-Kruger Effect

Overconfidence's most harmful result is lousy decision-making. And examples of poor decisions—the ones that make you scratch your head and say, "What the *hell* were they thinking?"—are legion.

Motorola owned 22% of the mobile phone market in the mid-2000s but failed to develop a smartphone until three years after Apple released the iPhone, with predictable consequences. Senior executives at 20th Century Fox agreed to give director George Lucas all of *Star Wars'* product and merchandising rights for only a $20,000 cut in Lucas's paycheck. Ross Perot's Electronic Data Systems (EDS) passed on buying Microsoft in 1979, and Blockbuster Video's then-CEO turned down acquiring Netflix in 2000. [121] [122] [123]

Overconfidence—also referred to in some instances as *Ego*—played a role in these decisions, exemplified by the last example and a revelation in Netflix co-founder Marc Randolph's book, *That Will Never Work*. Former Blockbuster CEO John Antioco turned down Netflix's offer to sell the company for $50 million because he "seemed to see it as a great big joke."

Antioco, who wore "loafers [that] probably cost more than my car," according to Randolph, had just swooped in and saved

Blockbuster from "a slide due to some poor business decisions. [...] He had not only turned Blockbuster's fortunes around, he'd led it through a successful IPO that raised $465 million the previous year." So, it's reasonable to speculate Blockbuster's CEO was riding high after a string of wins, and overconfidence blinded him to the opportunity and competitive reality sitting across the table. Of course, Blockbuster ceased corporate operations in 2014, while, as of this writing, Netflix is worth a bit under $300 billion. [124] [125]

A particularly insidious form of overconfidence is the Dunning-Kruger effect, a cognitive bias described by sociologists David Dunning and Justin Kruger. It happens when incompetent people overestimate their abilities, or highly competent people underestimate their abilities. Dunning and Kruger argue that "the miscalibration of the incompetent stems from an error about the self, whereas the miscalibration of the highly competent stems from an error about others." [126] [127]

Let's unpack this: some incompetent (or less competent people) think they are hot stuff because they overestimate their ability. And when they assume they're highly skilled, they often make poor decisions and get complacent about the need for self-improvement. In contrast, many competent individuals *think* they are perceived worse than they are—and this fear likely drives them to excel and improve.

Many people who cite the Dunning-Kruger effect forget that it covers both types of people, the incompetent and the competent, exclusively describing individuals who think they're way better at something than they are. It's easy to see why. At some point, almost everyone runs into an egotistical boss who makes poor decisions or a bureaucrat who confidently asserts something untrue. And a quick scan of social media or the comments under online articles and videos shows that one side of the Dunning-Kruger effect is thriving.

Everyday examples of the Dunning-Kruger effect include people who schedule far too many tasks and fail to accomplish most of them, individuals who can't take constructive criticism, and people who fake expertise on a subject while convincing themselves they have it. For example, in several studies, Dunning and his colleagues asked "respondents if they are familiar with a variety of terms related to subjects including politics, biology, physics, and geography. Along with genuine subject-relevant concepts, [the researchers] interjected **completely made-up terms**." In one of the studies, "approximately 90 percent of respondents claimed that they had at least some knowledge of the made-up terms." [128]

An observation by Professor Andy Yap from the INSEAD business school draws a bright line between the Dunning-Kruger effect and victory disease:

> "Employees who pretend too much sometimes, or fake it till they make it, they never make it and they continue to be unaware of that. If they have done it for a long time, this effect is going to be way stronger on them, because the cost of revealing (the truth) then is going to be higher. It's a sunk cost, and so they would rather like to keep up the pretense." He adds that honest negative feedback is becoming a rarity nowadays, contributing to a lack of accurate information about one's abilities. [...] If we don't reveal weaknesses, we never improve. We will never know what's the reality." [129]

Complacency and Following Established Patterns

At its core, victory disease is also a condition of complacency. An organization struggles, innovates, grows, and succeeds, usually followed by a significant period of steady success. Many steps that led to these wins are repeated—lacking in innovation—for years or even decades. It all works, for a time. The maxim "if it ain't broke, don't fix it" kicks in, and the organization eventually fails to see when things *have become* broken until the consequences pile up.

Most research on organizational complacency and the high-profile examples of its consequences involve risk management—avoiding dramatic, sudden, and often dangerous events.

Take the Deepwater Horizon disaster of 2010, "the largest marine oil spill in history." Its immediate cause was an explosion resulting from "a surge of natural gas" ripping through a faulty concrete core installed to seal an oil well in the Gulf of Mexico. The gas ignited after making its way up the riser of the Deepwater Horizon oil rig. The explosion killed 11 workers, injured 17 others, and capsized the rig, exposing a high-pressure gush of oil and causing one of the worst ecological disasters in history. In about three months, "approximately 134 million gallons of oil ... spilled into the ocean." [130] [131]

President Barack Obama formed a bipartisan commission to assess the disaster, and its investigators found avoidable, apparent mistakes that caused and worsened the spill.

> The panel's investigators uncovered "a suite of bad decisions," many still inexplicable, involving tests that were poorly run, alarming results that were ignored, proper equipment that was sidelined and safety barriers that were removed prematurely at the high-pressure well [...]

> A stream of evidence shows that "a culture of complacency" rather than a "culture of safety" prevailed at BP, Transocean Ltd. and Halliburton as they worked on the ill-fated Deepwater Horizon drilling rig.[132]

Complacency, along with groupthink and inept bureaucracy, was cited as a primary factor in the Chernobyl and Fukushima Daiichi nuclear meltdowns in 1986 and 2011, the deadly explosion of 2,750 tons of ammonium nitrate at the Port of Beirut in 2020, and many other international disasters. [133] [134] [135]

Complacency can affect all of us if we're not vigilant for its signs. Researchers at the University at Buffalo School of Management "studied ... post-disaster reports to assess why some people refused to evacuate in the face of warnings about imminent tornadoes, hurricanes and other emergency situations such as campus shootings and industrial accidents." They found that individuals with "past personal experience in 'riding out' storms" became complacent when authorities issued new warnings." [136]

When it comes to military conflict, we've seen how complacency affected the Japanese and US militaries. Japanese military leaders rigidly clung to a 40-year-old "Decisive Victory" strategy and 'coordinated, overwhelming strike' air tactics throughout World War II, both of which contributed to their defeat. And US leaders in Somalia allowed their enemy to discern repeatable patterns in Task Force Ranger's ground and air assaults, setting the stage for intense tactical resistance and US casualties that ultimately resulted in another strategic defeat for American foreign policy.

The high-profile examples of industrial disasters and military defeats may have life-and-death stakes, but they illustrate the cause of complacency in all settings. Humans and organizations fall into comfortable patterns because those actions are easy, show no signs of harm, and seem to maintain desired outcomes. There are warning signs, but those are rationalized, ignored, or swept under the rug. Not fixing what ain't broke nor rocking the boat becomes part of a toxic culture that leads to calamity.

Although it may seem unfathomable, some industrial or military leaders become complacent enough to disregard warnings and ignore risks that ultimately result in financial losses, tarnished reputations, and most gravely, **death.** So, what's stopping many business leaders from becoming complacent with even lower stakes?

It's one reason victory disease tends to be insidious. Everything seems fine on the surface for many years. But becoming complacent about external or internal threats rots the organization slowly from within, and the condition can destroy a company if it's not treated in time. Numerous business writers and analysts have accurately dubbed complacency a "silent business killer." [137] [138] [139] [140]

Research in Motion (RIM) is a widely cited example of the consequences of business complacency. The company innovated handheld computing in mobile phones by creating the incredibly successful Blackberry before inexplicably watching Apple leave its technology in the dust. Another example is Kodak, which mostly ignored digital cameras before going bankrupt in 2012—even though a Kodak engineer *invented* the technology 37 years before the company's demise. Kodak executives who viewed inventor Steven Sasson's prototype technology in 1975 told him they "were convinced that no one would ever want to look at their pictures on a television set" but let Sasson pursue the technology. When Sasson and a colleague built the first working DSLR camera fourteen years later, Kodak marketing executives saw the sales potential but didn't want to "cannibalize film sales." It's hard to think of a more stunning example of organizational complacency (and shortsighted stupidity). [141] [142]

Complacency shapes people and organizations into mediocre performers that lose critical thinking ability and competitiveness. At the organizational level, it's a fundamental cultural issue. Nevertheless, spotting the symptoms can be challenging because culture has two aspects: the things an organization *says* it is, and the factors that define what it *really* is. Business executive Torben Rick highlights the hidden impacts of culture with a useful iceberg illustration. Above the waterline are the public, idealized aspects of culture, including "policies," "shared values," "vision," "structure," and "strategy." Below the surface are "beliefs," "perceptions," "shared assumptions," "tradition," and "unwritten rules." It's an apt metaphor, as the hidden portion of an iceberg is much larger and more dangerous. [143]

Nevertheless, complacency can also manifest in highly public ways. For example, our review of GE's downward spiral in the previous chapter showed how the decline resulted from relentlessly chasing a well-known objective while using the same well-known strategy—even though conditions had changed. Complacency is often a hidden cultural rot that slowly weakens organizations and eventually takes them down in 'death by a thousand small cuts.' There may not be a singular event like a nuclear meltdown, an explosion that spills millions of gallons of oil, or smoldering and sinking aircraft carriers. But a slow-moving business disaster, often ending in Chapter 11 bankruptcy, is eventually assured.

Underestimating the "Enemy," Ignoring Intelligence, and the Ultimate Symptom of Victory Disease

Summaries of victory disease list **stereotyping and underestimating enemies** and **ignoring information that doesn't fit preconceptions** as additional symptoms. These aspects are common and dangerous, but they are *follow-on* symptoms of overconfidence and complacency.

For example, the British Army never thought the Japanese Army could take Singapore, dubbed "The Gibraltar of the East," let alone believed the Japanese could do it in a couple of weeks. Underestimating their enemy was a massive factor in this stunning defeat. Similarly, Japan misread its enemy's will to fight in World War II, as did the French and Americans in Vietnam. And US military planners underestimated the Somali fighters' ability to recognize patterns, organize, and put up a fight in Mogadishu. [144] [145]

Similarly, Dell misjudged the competition from HP, Nokia and Motorola underestimated Apple, Barnes and Noble underestimated Amazon, and all of the "world's leading telecommunications companies" underestimated Huawei. Each of these examples led to significant losses in market share, at a minimum. [146] [147]

The 1941 attack on Pearl Harbor, the 1967 Yom Kippur War, the 1968 Tet Offensive in Vietnam, and the 1978 Iranian Revolution all involved failing to see a situation for what it truly was, despite possessing valuable, revealing intelligence. Similarly, Borders', Polaroid's, Kodak's, and Blockbuster's failures to recognize that digital delivery was the inevitable future didn't stem from lack of intelligence; the signs were all there and pretty obvious. These organizations and others simply didn't recognize or use that intelligence quickly or successfully enough to innovate and compete. [148] [149]

Underestimating opponents and ignoring vital intelligence are common symptoms of victory disease. But these traits and more all stem from the two biggest factors: overconfidence and complacency after a period of success.

If you are a leader who can effect change in an organization showing these traits, *do it*. And if you are an employee who recognizes these symptoms but can't do anything about them, it might be a good idea to polish your resume.

CONCLUSION

Victory Disease can infect any organization. Wise leaders recognize this and refrain from thinking, "That could never happen in our company!" The fact is, as shown throughout this book, that this disease has and will continue to infect companies, large and small, in every industry and profession in Corporate America.

Companies that successfully avoid falling victim to this affliction will be those led by humble, agile-minded leaders who ensure prudent steps are taken to recognize and mitigate its symptoms and early warning signs.

Conversely, the companies who succumb to this infectious disease will be led by executives who are so blinded by their organizations' past successes and accolades they either cannot conceive of the possibility of failure, or as previously mentioned and seen in the examples provided in this book, their hubris and overconfidence is such that they simply reject the notion that it could ever happen to them.

I urge leaders to reflect upon the wisdom of the ancient Roman tradition in which victorious generals, while receiving the highest forms of praise and adulation, were reminded by a continuous whisper of warning that stated, *Memento Mori*

(Remember that you, too, will die), in an attempt to remind the conquering hero that he was still a mere mortal and to inspire him to remain humble.

Go Forth and Lead Well!

"In combat, complacency kills people.
In business, it kills companies."

– Mike Ettore

GRATITUDE

To Nancy,

A dear friend, confidant and source of wise counsel . . . the first person I called for help during one of the worst days of my life . . . always looking after my best interests . . . willing to tell me when my "great ideas" really aren't . . . I appreciate you and value your loyal friendship!

> *"Nothing, however, delights the mind as much*
> *as loving and loyal friendship."*
>
> *— Seneca*

Also by Mike Ettore

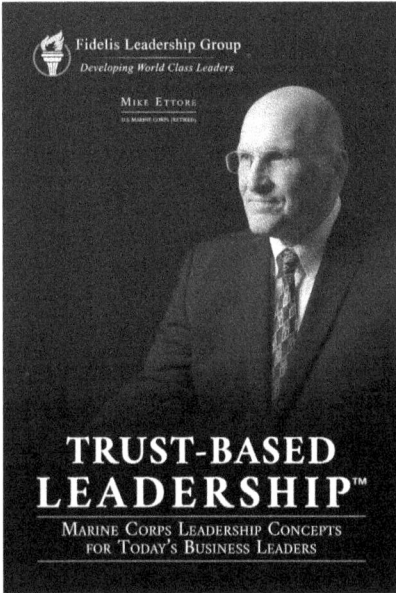

TRUST-BASED LEADERSHIP™:
Marine Corps Leadership
Concepts For Today's
Business Leaders

by Mike Ettore

ISBNs:
Paperback: 978-0-9898229-4-7
Hardcover: 978-0-9898229-8-5
Ebook: 978-0-9898229-5-4

Available at:
Amazon, Barnes&Noble.com, Kindle, iBooks, and many other retailers

This 574 page book details how the author effectively adapted and applied Marine Corps leadership concepts while serving as a business leader— and how he leverages the Trust-Based Leadership™ model to help others become World-Class Leaders.

Section I – Marine Corps Leadership
Section II – Trust-Based Leadership™
Section III – The Trust-Based Leader
Section IV – Lessons Learned
Section V – Leadership Articles

Mike is highly regarded for his unique ability to help leaders rapidly elevate their skills as they create and sustain high-performance teams. He wrote this book to help leaders at all levels maximize their potential and become World Class Leaders.

Also by Mike Ettore

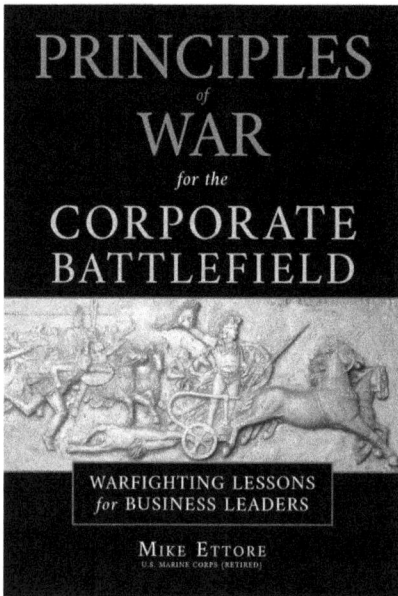

PRINCIPLES OF WAR FOR THE CORPORATE BATTLE-FIELD: Warfighting Lessons for Business Leaders

by Mike Ettore

ISBNs:
Paperback: 978-0-9898229-9-2
Hardcover: 978-1-7372881-0-7
Ebook: 978-1-7372881-1-4

Available at:
Amazon, Barnes&Noble.com, Kindle, iBooks, and many other retailers

The "missions" of the business battlefield are not dissimilar from actual military battlefields . . . establishing the desired end state, describing and assigning the necessary tasks, designing and task-organizing the unit to best support mission accomplishment, assembling and developing the team, and achieving operational unity of effort via timely and precise communications.

The risks associated with both battlefields are similar as well. It is almost inevitable that soldiers may die or become wounded in combat and their units may suffer loss. Likewise, a company may fail and place the livelihoods and welfare its employees at great risk. While this does not bring forth the physical risks associated with war, business failures are personally damaging and the negative effects are lasting.

This book contains examples of how each principle has been successfully applied in both military and business environments, and it **will enable business leaders to quickly and effectively apply The Principles of War in their own planning and operations.**

Also by Mike Ettore

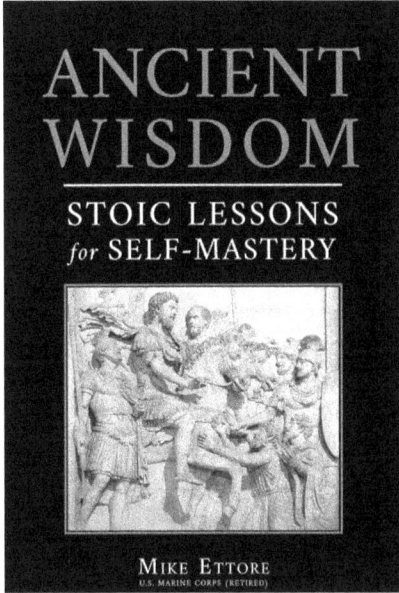

ANCIENT WISDOM:
Stoic Lessons for Self-Mastery

by Mike Ettore

ISBNs:
Paperback: 978-1-7372881-3-8
Hardcover: 978-1-7372881-2-1
Ebook: 978-1-7372881-4-5

Available at:
Amazon, Barnes&Noble.com, Kindle,
iBooks, and many other retailers

Frederick the Great, George Washington, Theodore Roosevelt, and many of today's most notable leaders, intellectuals, and high achievers learned to embrace the wisdom of the ancient Stoics as they sought to live happy, successful, and productive lives.

This book uniquely combines insights from Marcus Aurelius, Seneca, Epictetus and other Stoic philosophers with the author's interpretations, musings, and life-time of experiences and lessons learned. The result is an easy-to-read book containing timeless wisdom and empowering advice that can help readers learn how to dramatically alter and control their emotional responses to life's inevitable challenges and obstacles.

Bonus Resources

↧

Download Your Bonus Resources!

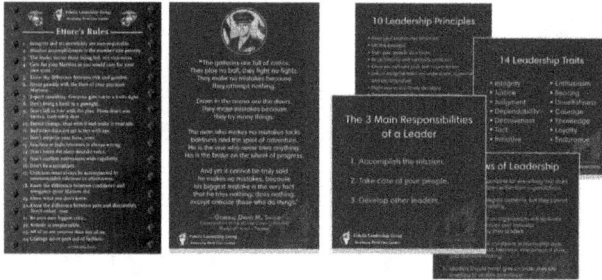

The graphics used in *Principles of War for the Corporate Battlefield* and *Trust-Based Leadership*™ and additional resources are available for free in the Bonus Resource Vault, which you can find at:

HTTPS://FIDELISLEADERSHIP.COM/BOOKBONUS

Social Media – Let's Stay In Touch!

🎙 **Fidelis Leadership Podcast:** https://www.fidelisleadership.com/podcast

📘 **Facebook**

- Fidelis: www.facebook.com/FidelisLeadershipGroup
- Mike: www.facebook.com/EttoreMike

🔗 **Linkedin:**

- Fidelis: www.linkedin.com/company/fidelis-leadership-group-llc
- Mike: www.linkedin.com/in/mikeettore/

🐦 **Twitter:** https://twitter.com/FidelisLeader

📷 **Instagram:** www.instagram.com/fidelisleadership/

Fidelis Leadership Newsletter

Receive monthly emails containing valuable lessons, tactics and techniques that can help you become a World-Class Leader! I promise that I will never share your contact information in any way, and if you decide to stop receiving the newsletter you can unsubscribe with one click.

SIGN UP NOW! HTTPS://FIDELISLEADERSHIP.COM

Fidelis Leadership Group

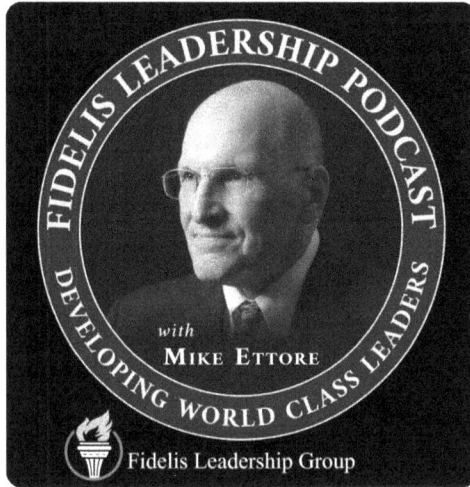

"A PLACE OF LEARNING FOR THOSE ASPIRING TO LEADERSHIP EXCELLENCE!"

The Fidelis Leadership Podcast is for those who want to become World Class Leaders. Weekly episodes convey lessons and advice from some of the world's foremost leadership experts, and discussions regarding the effective application of the Trust-Based Leadership™ model.

HTTPS://WWW.FIDELISLEADERSHIP.COM/PODCAST

Also Found on Your Favorite Podcast Platforms!

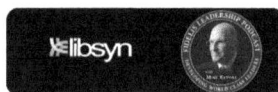

From the Author

Book Reviews

Thank you for reading my book. Please consider visiting the site where you purchased it and writing a brief review. Your feedback is important to me and will help others decide whether to read the book too.

New Books, Training Programs and Events

If you'd like to get notifications of my latest books, training programs and leadership events, please join my email list by visiting https://fidelisleadership.com

Bulk Purchase Discounts

If you would like to purchase 25 or more print copies of this book, we are happy to offer you a discount on the net list price of the book. Please send inquiries to: info@fidelisleadership.com

Fidelis Leadership Group
Developing World Class Leaders

My Services

Executive Coaching

My executive coaching engagements are uniquely tailored to each individual and are designed to provide focus that can deepen an executive's self-awareness and promote personal and professional growth. The private coaching sessions provide leaders with an opportunity to engage in focused, constructive, and confidential dialogue with a skilled and objective listener. I collaborate with each leader to design a program that fosters and accelerates individual growth, while providing the coaching and facilitation to achieve desired outcomes.

Leadership Development

I help educate, train, and coach leaders so they can dramatically accelerate their personal and professional development. I work best with clients who operate in a culture of execution, accountability, and leadership by example—or those who desire to create such a culture within their organizations. I offer customized leadership training and development programs—including onsite training seminars - for leaders at every level: C-Suite and SVP-VP-Director level, high-potential individuals and others serving in mid-level and front-line leadership roles.

Speaking

I am an experienced public speaker with a strong history of delivering dynamic, interactive, and memorable presentations and keynote speeches to a wide range of organizations. Leveraging leadership lessons that were forged in the unforgiving crucible of combat and while serving as a senior executive, I inspire and energize my audiences and provide them with actionable strategies, tactics, and techniques that they can implement immediately upon returning to their teams.

CONTACT ME NOW!
info@fidelisleadership.com

ENDNOTES

1   Conrad, Sebastian (2014). "The Dialectics of Remembrance: Memories of Empire in Cold War Japan" (PDF). Comparative Studies in Society and History. 56 (1): 8. https://core.ac.uk/download/pdf/199424523.pdf

2   James, David H. "The Rise and Fall of the Japanese Empire."

3   Egan, Matt. "General Electric gets booted from the Dow." CNN Business. https://money.cnn.com/2018/06/19/investing/ge-dow-jones-walgreens/index.html

4   "General Electric - 58 Year Stock Price History | GE." macrotrends. https://www.macrotrends.net/stocks/charts/GE/general-electric/stock-price-history

5   Stony Brook University. "Success breeds success, study confirms." ScienceDaily. www.sciencedaily.com/releases/2014/04/140428154838.htm (accessed December 9, 2020).

6   Lee, Terry. "'Only the Paranoid Survive' Review." Medium. https://medium.com/@terryjohnlee/only-the-paranoid-survive-review-744d6b453e40

7   Duffy, James P. "War at the End of the World: Douglas MacArthur and the Forgotten Fight For New Guinea, 1942-1945." Penguin 2016. https://books.google.com/books?id=PgUXCAAAQBAJ&pg=PT66&lpg=PT66&dq=-senshoubyou&source=bl&ots=fFgIfgcn_5&sig=ACfU3U31ISo0J43W6BEn-NbuC4ciF7ErJZw&hl=en&sa=X&ved=2ahUKEwj29eWk6cjtAhVpu1kKHY-alDsM4ChDoATAEegQIBRAC#v=onepage&q=senshoubyou&f=false

8   The Editors of Encyclopaedia Britannica. "Empire of Japan." Encyclopaedia Britannica. https://www.britannica.com/place/Empire-of-Japan

9   Witzke, Mark. "How Much of China did Japan Control at its Greatest Extent?" Pacific Atrocities Education. https://www.pacificatrocities.org/blog/how-much-of-china-did-japan-control-at-its-greatest-extent

10   Hoadley, Stephen and Ruland, Jurgen (editors). "Asian Security Reassessed." Institute of Southeast Asian Studies (2006). pp. 48-49, 63, ISBN 981-230-400-2   https://books.google.com/books?id=5P9bgGxfYKUC&p-g=PA63&dq=%22new+order+of+east+asia%22+%22greater+east+a-sia+co-prosperity%22&hl=en&ei=B8TXTs3aHvT64QSoj4GHDg&sa=X-&oi=book_result&ct=result&resnum=4&ved=0CD0Q6AEwAw#v=onep-age&q=%22new%20order%20of%20east%20asia%22%20%22greater%20east%20asia%20co-prosperity%22&f=false

11   Graham, James. "Japan's Economic Expansion into Manchuria and China in World War Two." On This Day. https://www.onthisday.com/asia/japan_economic_expansion.php

12   Higgs, Robert. "How U.S. Economic Warfare Provoked Japan's Attack on Pearl Harbor." Independent Institute. https://www.independent.org/news/article.asp?id=1930

13   "Why Japan Really Lost The War." Imperial Japanese Navy Page. http://www.combinedfleet.com/economic.htm

14   Cohen, Eliot. "Kaigun: Strategy, Tactics, and Technology in the Imperial Japanese Navy, 1887-1941." Foreign Affairs. https://www.foreignaffairs.com/reviews/capsule-review/1998-05-01/kaigun-strategy-tactics-and-technology-imperial-japanese-navy

15   "Decisive Battle Doctrine." The Pacific War Online Encyclopedia. http://pwencycl.kgbudge.com/D/e/Decisive_Battle_Doctrine.htm

16   History.com Editors. "Pearl Harbor." History.com. https://www.history.com/topics/world-war-ii/pearl-harbor

17   Alison. "Pearl Harbor's Oil Tank: What Could Have Been." PearlHarbor.Org. https://pearlharbor.org/pearl-harbors-third-strike-what-could-have-been/

18   History.com Editors. "Pearl Harbor." History.com. https://www.history.com/topics/world-war-ii/pearl-harbor

19   Primus V. "Lessons in Surprise." Harvard Magazine. https://harvardmagazine.com/2010/07/lessons-in-surprise

20   Hughes, Thomas A. "Yamamoto Isoroku." Encyclopaedia Britannica. https://www.britannica.com/biography/Yamamoto-Isoroku

21   Fumimaro Konoe, Konoye Ayamaro Ko Shuki (Memoirs of Prince Ayamaro Konoye), Asahi Shimbun-sha, 1946, p. 3.

22   Royde-Smith, John Graham. World War II: 1939-1945. Encyclopædia Britannica. https://www.britannica.com/event/World-War-II

23   Hickman, Kennedy. "The History of World War II's Battle of Singapore." ThoughtCo. https://www.thoughtco.com/world-war-ii-battle-of-singapore-2361472

24   "Japan's Territorial Expansion 1931-1942." Stratfor. https://worldview.stratfor.com/article/japans-territorial-expansion-1931-1942

25   "Doolittle Raid." Naval History and Heritage Command. https://www.history.navy.mil/browse-by-topic/wars-conflicts-and-operations/world-war-ii/1942/halsey-doolittle-raid.html

26   Array. "Aftermath: How the Doolittle Raid Shook Japan." HistoryNet. https://www.historynet.com/aftermath-doolittle-raid-reexamined.htm

27   "Operation MO and the Battle of the Coral Sea." Stuff. http://www.stuff.co.nz/national/last-post-first-light/our-anzacs-stories/6860260/Operation-MO-and-the-Battle-of-the-Coral-Sea

28   History.com Editors. "Battle of Coral Sea." https://www.history.com/topics/world-war-ii/battle-of-coral-sea

29   Ray, Michael. "The Battle of Midway." Encyclopaedia Britannica https://www.britannica.com/event/Battle-of-Midway

30   History.com Editors. "Battle of Midway." History.com. https://www.history.com/topics/world-war-ii/battle-of-midway

31   "Index to the Battle of Midway, 4 - 6 June 1942." The Pacific War Historical Society. https://www.pacificwar.org.au/Midway/MidwayIndex.html

32   Ray, Michael. "The Battle of Midway." Encyclopaedia Britannica https://www.britannica.com/event/Battle-of-Midway

33   "Battle of Midway." 2007 Schools Wikipedia Selection. https://www.cs.mcgill.ca/~rwest/wikispeedia/wpcd/wp/b/Battle_of_Midway.htm

34   "General Electric." *Encyclopaedia Britannica*. https://www.britannica.com/topic/General-Electric

35   Reed, Eric. "General Electric's History and Future." *TheStreet*. https://www.thestreet.com/markets/general-electric-history-future-14791857

36   GE Reports Staff. "5 Things You Didn't Know About Brilliant Innovation at GE." GE.com. https://www.ge.com/news/reports/5-things-didnt-know-brilliant-innovation-ge

37   Taylor, Brian. "General Electric: The Fallen Giant." Investment Office. https://www.investmentoffice.com/Observations/Capital_Markets/General_Electric_The_Fallen_Giant.html

38   Barr, Colin. "Meet the market's biggest losers." Fortune. https://archive.fortune.com/galleries/2010/fortune/1002/gallery.biggest_losers.fortune/2.html

39   Colvin, Geoffrey."The Ultimate Manager In a time of hidebound, formulaic thinking, General Electric's Jack Welch gave power to the worker and the shareholder. He built one hell of a company in the process." Fortune via CNN Money. https://money.cnn.com/magazines/fortune/fortune_archive/1999/11/22/269126/index.htm

40   Huang, Nellie S. "The World's Biggest Companies Over the Past 20 Years." Kiplinger. https://www.kiplinger.com/slideshow/investing/t052-s001-the-world-s-biggest-companies-over-the-past-20-yea/index.html

41   Colvin, Geoffrey. "The Ultimate Manager In a time of hidebound, formulaic thinking, General Electric's Jack Welch gave power to the worker and the shareholder. He built one hell of a company in the process." Fortune via CNN Money. https://money.cnn.com/magazines/fortune/fortune_archive/1999/11/22/269126/index.htm

42   Nocera, Joe. "Was Jack Welch Really That Good?" Bloomberg Businessweek. https://www.bloomberg.com/news/articles/2019-06-12/reassessing-jack-welch-s-legacy-after-ge-s-decline-joe-nocera

43   Colvin, Geoffrey. "The Ultimate Manager In a time of hidebound, formulaic thinking, General Electric's Jack Welch gave power to the worker and the shareholder. He built one hell of a company in the process." Fortune via CNN Money. https://money.cnn.com/magazines/fortune/fortune_archive/1999/11/22/269126/index.htm

44   Schrager, James E. "Three strategy lessons from GE's decline." ChicagoBooth Review. https://review.chicagobooth.edu/strategy/2019/article/three-strategy-lessons-ge-s-decline

45   Lohr, Steve. "Jack Welch, G.E. Chief Who Became a Business Superstar, Dies at 84." The New York Times. https://www.nytimes.com/2020/03/02/business/jack-welch-died.html

46   Schrager, James E. "Three strategy lessons from GE's decline." Chicago Booth Review. https://review.chicagobooth.edu/strategy/2019/article/three-strategy-lessons-ge-s-decline

47   "Jack Welch, GE Chief Who Made Bold Acquisition of RCA, NBC, Dies At 84." Associated Press. https://www.pbs.org/newshour/economy/former-ge-ceo-jack-welch-dies-at-84

48   Vise, David A. "GE to Buy RCA for $6.2 Billion." The Washington Post. https://www.washingtonpost.com/archive/politics/1985/12/12/ge-to-buy-rca-for-62-billion/9d2145e1-3621-466e-93d0-592055310652/

49   Tong, Scott. "Jack Welch's legacy: value for shareholders, but not necessarily for workers." Marketplace. https://www.marketplace.org/2020/03/02/jack-welchs-legacy-value-for-shareholders-but-not-necessarily-for-workers/

50   Mont, Joe. "10 CEOs Who Became 'Job Killers.'" TheStreet. https://www.thestreet.com/personal-finance/10-ceos-who-became-job-killers-12789065

51   "Jack Welch." Reference for Business. https://www.referenceforbusiness.com/businesses/G-L/Welch-Jack.html

52   Ashkenas, Ron, DeMonaco, Lawrence J., and Francis, Suzanne. "Making the Deal Real: How GE Capital Integrates Acquisitions." Harvard Business Review. https://hbr.org/1998/01/making-the-deal-real-how-ge-capital-integrates-acquisitions

53   Colvin, Geoffrey. "GE under siege." CNN Money. https://money.cnn.com/2008/10/09/news/companies/colvin_ge.fortune/index.htm

54   Forbes, Steve. "Jack Welch: Managerial Genius Who Made One Disastrous Mistake." Forbes. https://www.forbes.com/sites/steveforbes/2020/03/03/jack-welch-managerial-genius-who-made-one-disastrous-mistake/?sh=3530f7533749

55   Van Dango, Dexter. "GE Capital: The House that Jack Built." monitordaily. https://www.monitordaily.com/article-posts/ge-capital-the-house-that-jack-built/

56   Colvin, Geoffrey. "GE under siege." CNN Money. https://money.cnn.com/2008/10/09/news/companies/colvin_ge.fortune/index.htm

57   Spross, Jeff. "Jack Welch's legacy looks very different than it did 20 years ago." The Week. https://theweek.com/articles/899343/jack-welchs-legacy-looks-different-than-did-20-years-ago

58   Swoboda, Frank. "GE Picks Welch's Successor." The Washington Post. https://www.washingtonpost.com/archive/business/2000/11/28/ge-picks-welchs-successor/8a0ecc0b-4273-42bd-b90e-0b1d5d493a3e/

59   Gelles, David. "Jeff Immelt Oversaw the Downfall of G.E. Now He'd Like You to Read His Book." The New York Times. https://www.nytimes.com/2021/02/05/business/jeff-immelt-general-electric-corner-office.html

60   Belvedere, Matthew J. "Ex-director Ken Langone: GE's 'destruction' happened after Jack Welch and it could now be 'busted up'." CNBC. https://www.cnbc.com/2018/02/28/ken-langone-ge-destruction-happened-after-jack-welch-left-as-ceo.html

61   Egan, Matt. "GE's $31 billion pension nightmare." CNN Business. https://money.cnn.com/2018/01/18/investing/ge-pension-immelt-break-up/index.html

62   Gryta, Thomas. "GE Won't Try to Claw Back Jeff Immelt's Pay." The Wall Street Journal. https://www.wsj.com/articles/ge-wont-try-to-claw-back-jeff-immelts-pay-11609878115

63   Gelles, David. "Jeff Immelt Oversaw the Downfall of G.E. Now He'd Like You to Read His Book." The New York Times. https://www.nytimes.com/2021/02/05/business/jeff-immelt-general-electric-corner-office.html

64   Bromels, John. "I Still Can't Believe General Electric Spent More Than $10 Billion for Alstom Power." The Motley Fool. https://www.fool.com/investing/2018/09/01/i-still-cant-believe-general-electric-spent-more-t.aspx

65   Ausick, Paul. "Why GE's Alstom Acquisition Was Misguided." 24/7 Wall St. https://247wallst.com/industrials/2019/06/07/why-ges-alstom-acquisition-was-misguided/

66   Egan, Matt. "How decades of bad decisions broke GE." CNN Business. https://money.cnn.com/2017/11/20/investing/general-electric-immelt-what-went-wrong/index.html

67   Schrager, James E. "Three strategy lessons from GE's decline." Chicago Booth Review. https://review.chicagobooth.edu/strategy/2019/article/three-strategy-lessons-ge-s-decline

68   Byrne, John A. "Jack Welch successor destroyed GE he inherited." USA Today. https://www.usatoday.com/story/opinion/2018/07/15/ge-ceo-welch-oppose-editorials-debates/36895027/

69   "The Rise and Fall of the Somali State." Stratfor. https://worldview.stratfor.com/article/rise-and-fall-somali-state

70   The Editors of Encyclopaedia Britannica. "Somali Civil War." Encyclopaedia Britannica. https://www.britannica.com/place/Somalia/Civil-war

71   Hogg, Annabel Lee. "Timeline: Somalia, 1991-2008." The Atlantic. https://www.theatlantic.com/magazine/archive/2008/12/timeline-somalia-1991-2008/307190/

72   The Editors of Encyclopaedia Britannica. "Somalia intervention." Encyclopaedia Britannica. https://www.britannica.com/event/Somalia-intervention

73   "U.S. Marines storm Mogadishu, Somalia." History.com. https://www.history.com/this-day-in-history/u-s-marines-storm-mogadishu-somalia

74   "Operation Restore Hope." GlobalSecurity.org. https://www.globalsecurity.org/military/ops/restore_hope.htm

75   "Unified Task Force." Wikipedia. https://en.wikipedia.org/wiki/Unified_Task_Force

76   "The United States Army in Somalia 1992-1994." US Army Center of Military History. https://history.army.mil/brochures/Somalia/Somalia.htm

77   Karcher, Timothy. "Understanding the "Victory Disease," From the Little Bighorn to Mogadishu and Beyond." Combat Studies Institute Press Fort Leavenworth, Kansas.

78   "United States Forces, Somalia: After Action Report." Center of Military History, United States Army. https://history.army.mil/html/documents/somalia/SomaliaAAR.pdf

79   Karcher, Timothy. "Understanding the "Victory Disease," From the Little Bighorn to Mogadishu and Beyond." Combat Studies Institute Press Fort Leavenworth, Kansas.

80   "United States Forces, Somalia: After Action Report." Center of Military History, United States Army. https://history.army.mil/html/documents/somalia/SomaliaAAR.pdf

81   Karcher, Timothy. "Understanding the "Victory Disease," From the Little Bighorn to Mogadishu and Beyond." Combat Studies Institute Press Fort Leavenworth, Kansas.

82   "United States Forces, Somalia: After Action Report." Center of Military History, United States Army. https://history.army.mil/html/documents/somalia/SomaliaAAR.pdf

83   King, Samuel. "Rangers remember with Mogadishu Mile." Eglin Air Force Base. https://www.eglin.af.mil/News/Article-Display/Article/2371726/rangers-remember-with-mogadishu-mile/

84   "Ambush in Mogadishu." PBS Frontline. https://www.pbs.org/wgbh/pages/frontline/shows/ambush/etc/synopsis.html

85   Karcher, Timothy. "Understanding the "Victory Disease," From the Little Bighorn to Mogadishu and Beyond." Combat Studies Institute Press Fort Leavenworth, Kansas.

86   Richburg, Keith B. "IN WAR ON AIDEED, U.N. BATTLED ITSELF." The Washington Post. https://www.washingtonpost.com/ archive/politics/1993/12/06/in-war-on-aideed-un-battled-itself/ a42feae5-4aff-4cd1-b680-8ee67c586a47/

87   Bunkley, Nick. "Ford Loses Record $12.7 Billion in '06." The New York Times. https://www.nytimes.com/2007/01/25/business/25cnd-ford.html

88   Hammond, Lou Ann. "How Ford did it." Fortune. https://archive. fortune.com/2011/01/12/autos/Bill-Ford-Alan-Mulally-carmaker.fortune/ index.htm

89   Singh, Ayush. "Here's Why Ford Motor Company Still Can't Avoid Bankruptcy." CCN. https://www.ccn.com/heres-why-ford-motor-company-still-cant-avoid-bankruptcy/

90   Almond, Jordan. "Is Ford Going Out of Business?" MotorBiscuit. https://www.motorbiscuit.com/is-ford-going-out-of-business

91   Farquhar, Dave. "Why did Apple fail in the 90s?" The Silicon Underground. https://dfarq.homeip.net/why-did-apple-fail-in-the-90s/

92   Lee, Timothy B. "How Apple became the world's most valuable company." Vox. https://www.vox.com/2014/11/17/18076360/apple

93   "Top 100 Retailers 2018." National Retail Federation. https://nrf.com/ resources/top-retailers/top-100-retailers/top-100-retailers-2018

94   McDowell, Erin. "The rise and fall of Sears, once the largest and most powerful retailer in the world." Business Insider. https://www.businessinsider.com/rise-and-fall-of-sears-bankruptcy-store-closings

95   "Global retail sales of Sears Holdings from 2005 to 2020." Statistia. https:// www.statista.com/statistics/292990/global-revenue-of-sears-holdings/

96   Comen, Evan. "Sears' Edward Lampert Is the Most Hated CEO in America." 24/7 Wall Street. https://247wallst.com/retail/2016/11/06/ sears-edward-lampert-is-the-most-hated-ceo-in-america/

97   Hirsch, Lauren and Thomas, Lauren. "Sears files for bankruptcy, and Eddie Lampert steps down as CEO." CNBC. https://www.cnbc. com/2018/10/15/sears-files-for-bankruptcy.html

98   Hirsch, Lauren. "Eddie Lampert's deal to buy Sears granted approval, as retailer is given a second life." CNBC. https://www.cnbc.com/2019/02/07/eddie-lamperts-deal-to-buy-sears-approved-retailer-given-second-life.html

99   "Top 100 Retailers 2021 List." National Retail Federation. https://nrf.com/resources/top-retailers/top-100-retailers/top-100-retailers-2021-list

100   Delventhal, Shoshanna. "Who Killed Sears? Fifty Years on the Road to Ruin." Investopedia. https://www.investopedia.com/news/downfall-of-sears/

101   McKinnon, Tricia. "The Downfall of Sears, 5 Reasons Why it's Struggling to Survive." Indigo9Digital. https://www.indigo9digital.com/blog/failureofsears

102   McKinnon, Tricia. "The Downfall of Sears, 5 Reasons Why it's Struggling to Survive." Indigo9Digital. https://www.indigo9digital.com/blog/failureofsears

103   Biron, Bethany and McDowell, Erin. "Inside the wild and tumultuous history of Toys R Us, a once beloved children's brand that just closed its last 2 stores in the US." Business Insider. https://www.businessinsider.com/the-tumultuous-history-of-toys-r-us-photos-2020-8

104   Ibid.

105   Verdon, Joan. "Toys R Us timeline: History of the nation's top toy chain." USA Today. https://www.usatoday.com/story/money/business/2018/03/09/toys-r-us-timeline-history-nations-top-toy-chain/409230002/

106   Blakemore, Erin. "Inside the Rise and Fall of Toys 'R' Us." History.com. https://www.history.com/news/toys-r-us-closing-legacy

107   Covert, Bryce. "The Demise of Toys 'R' Us Is a Warning." The Atlantic. https://www.theatlantic.com/magazine/archive/2018/07/toys-r-us-bankruptcy-private-equity/561758/

108   "The Downfall of Toys R Us — Don't Blame Amazon!" Brand Minds. https://brand-minds.medium.com/the-downfall-of-toys-r-us-dont-blame-amazon-c88856516383

109   Blakemore, Erin. "Inside the Rise and Fall of Toys 'R' Us." History.com. https://www.history.com/news/toys-r-us-closing-legacy

110   "What Went Wrong: The Demise of Toys R Us." Knowledge@Wharton. https://knowledge.wharton.upenn.edu/article/the-demise-of-toys-r-us/

111   Ibid.

112   Lucas, Clay. "Confidence linked to success in workplace." The Sydney Morning Herald. https://www.smh.com.au/lifestyle/confidence-linked-to-success-in-workplace-20121017-27rlf.html

113   Kay, Katty and Shipman, Claire. "The Confidence Gap." The Atlantic. https://www.theatlantic.com/magazine/archive/2014/05/the-confidence-gap/359815/

114   Nasher, Jack. "To Seem More Competent, Be More Confident." Harvard Business Review. https://hbr.org/2019/03/to-seem-more-competent-be-more-confident

115   "Confidence can change others' perception of an individual's success: study." CTV. https://www.ctvnews.ca/health/confidence-can-change-others-perception-of-an-individual-s-success-study-1.1982488

116   Ackerman, Courtney E. "What is Self-Efficacy Theory in Psychology?" PositivePsychology.com. https://positivepsychology.com/self-efficacy/

117   Briggs, Saga. "Why Self-Esteem Hurts Learning But Self-Confidence Does The Opposite." informED. https://www.opencolleges.edu.au/informed/features/self-efficacy-and-learning/

118   Baumeister, Roy F., Campbell, Jennifer D., Krueger, Joachim I., and Vohs, Kathleen D. "Does High Self-Esteem Cause Better Performance, Interpersonal Success, Happiness, or Healthier Lifestyles?" Psychological Science in the Public Interest. Volume: 4 issue: 1, page(s): 1-44, May 1, 2003.

119   "Too low and too high self-confidence do not lead to career success." Do Better by Esade. https://dobetter.esade.edu/en/self-confidence-career-success?_wrapper_format=html

120   "Too low and too high self-confidence do not lead to career success." Do Better by esade. https://dobetter.esade.edu/en/self-confidence-career-success?_wrapper_format=html

121   Anderson, Erika. "It Seemed Like A Good Idea At The Time: 7 Of The Worst Business Decisions Ever Made." Forbes. https://www.forbes.com/sites/erikaandersen/2013/10/04/it-seemed-like-a-good-idea-at-the-time-7-of-the-worst-business-decisions-ever-made/?sh=7e9abfc03e80

122   "8 Of The Worst Business Decisions Ever Made." CEO Today. https://www.ceotodaymagazine.com/2018/08/8-of-the-worst-business-decisions-ever-made/

123   Zetlin, Minda. "Blockbuster Could Have Bought Netflix for $50 Million, but the CEO Thought It Was a Joke." Inc. https://www.inc.com/minda-zetlin/netflix-blockbuster-meeting-marc-randolph-reed-hastings-john-antioco.html

124   Ibid.

125   Bowman, Cynthia. "How Much Is Netflix Worth?" Go Banking Rates. https://www.gobankingrates.com/money/business/how-much-is-netflix-worth/

126   Kruger, Justin; Dunning, David (1999). "Unskilled and Unaware of It: How Difficulties in Recognizing One's Own Incompetence Lead to Inflated Self-Assessments." Journal of Personality and Social Psychology. 77 (6): 1121–1134.

127   Cherry, Kendra. "The Dunning-Kruger Effect." Verywellmind. https://www.verywellmind.com/an-overview-of-the-dunning-kruger-effect-4160740

128   Ibid.

129   Lai, Leila. "Not so blissful ignorance: The Dunning-Kruger effect at work." The Business Times. https://www.businesstimes.com.sg/brunch/not-so-blissful-ignorance-the-dunning-kruger-effect-at-work

130   Pallardy, Richard. "Deepwater Horizon oil spill." Encyclopædia Britannica. https://www.britannica.com/event/Deepwater-Horizon-oil-spill

131   "Oil spills." National Oceanic and Atmospheric Administration. https://www.noaa.gov/education/resource-collections/ocean-coasts/oil-spills

132   Banerjee, Veela. "Investigators see 'culture of complacency' behind gulf oil spill." The Los Angeles Times. https://www.latimes.com/archives/la-xpm-2010-nov-10-la-na-oil-spill-commission-20101110-story.html

133   "On Chernobyl anniversary, Amano warns against complacency, vows IAEA will help prevent nuclear disasters." The Japan Times. https://www.japantimes.co.jp/news/2016/04/27/national/science-health/chernobyl-anniversary-amano-warns-complacency-vows-iaea-will-help-prevent-nuclear-disasters/

134   "Complacency contributed to Fukushima accident, says Amano." World Nuclear News. https://www.world-nuclear-news.org/RS-Complacency-contributed-to-Fukushima-accident-says-Amano-0209154.html

135   "Beirut explosion: Lebanon in mourning as international assistance arrives." Deutsche Welle. https://www.dw.com/en/beirut-explosion-lebanon-in-mourning-as-international-assistance-arrives/a-54456502

136   Wilde, Cathy. "Complacency, apathy lead people to ignore disaster warnings, researchers say." University of Buffalo News Center. http://www.buffalo.edu/news/releases/2013/06/048.html

137   Swyers, Matthew. Inc. "Is Your Business Suffering From This Silent Killer?" https://www.inc.com/matthew-swyers/complacency-the-silent-business-killer.html

138   "Complacency is a Company Killer." Axiom Strategic Consulting. https://www.axiomstrategic.com/blog/complacency-is-a-company-killer

139   Rick, Torben. "THE SILENT BUSINESS KILLER – ORGANIZATIONAL COMPLACENCY IS THE ENEMY OF SUCCESS." Meliorate. https://www.tor-benrick.eu/blog/culture/the-silent-business-killer/

140   Ruisi, Chris. "Complacency: The Silent Business Killer." American Express Business Class. https://www.americanexpress.com/en-us/business/trends-and-insights/articles/complacency-silent-business-killer/

141   Linder, Markus. "What Have You Done For Me Lately? Business Leaders, Don't Become Complacent." Business 2 Community. https://www.business2community.com/marketing/what-have-you-done-for-me-lately-business-leaders-dont-become-complacent-02082912

142   McAlone, Nathan. "This man invented the digital camera in 1975 — and his bosses at Kodak never let it see the light of day." Business Insider. https://www.businessinsider.com/this-man-invented-the-digital-camera-in-1975-and-his-bosses-at-kodak-never-let-it-see-the-light-of-day-2015-8

143   Rick, Torben. "THE SILENT BUSINESS KILLER – ORGANIZATIONAL COMPLACENCY IS THE ENEMY OF SUCCESS." Meliorate. https://www.tor-benrick.eu/blog/culture/the-silent-business-killer/

144   Steward, Oliver. "The fall of Singapore: An avoidable catastrophe?" The UK Defence Journal. https://ukdefencejournal.org.uk/the-fall-of-singapore-an-avoidable-catastrophe/

145   Knighton, Andrew. "Underestimating the Enemy – The French Military Disaster At Dien Bien Phu." War History Online. https://www.warhistoryonline.com/vietnam-war/8-reasons-french-military-disaster-di-en-bien_phu-mmm.html

146   "9 Companies That Destroyed Their Largest Competitors." 24/7 Wall St. via Business Insider. https://www.businessinsider.com/nine-companies-that-destroyed-their-largest-competitors-2011-8

147   Ryans, Adrian. "When companies underestimate low-cost rivals." McKinsey & Company. https://www.mckinsey.com/business-functions/strategy-and-corporate-finance/our-insights/when-companies-underestimate-low-cost-rivals

148   Goh, Frances. "10 COMPANIES THAT FAILED TO INNOVATE, RESULTING IN BUSINESS FAILURE." Collective Campus. https://www.collectivecampus.io/blog/10-companies-that-were-too-slow-to-respond-to-change

149   Thangavelu, Poonkulali. "Companies That Failed to Innovate and Went Bankrupt." Investopedia. https://www.investopedia.com/articles/investing/072115/companies-went-bankrupt-innovation-lag.asp

www.ingramcontent.com/pod-product-compliance
Lightning Source LLC
Chambersburg PA
CBHW050645190326
41458CB00008B/2427